WAKE ISLAND

Considering the power accumulated for the invasion of Wake Island, and the meager forces of the defenders, it was one of the most humiliating defeats we had ever suffered.

Masatake Okumiya, Commander
Japanese Imperial Navy

WAKE ISLAND

The Heroic, Gallant Fight

Duane Schultz

St. Martin's Press   New York

Copyright © 1978 by Duane Schultz
All rights reserved. For information, write:
St. Martin's Press, Inc., 175 Fifth Ave., New York, N.Y. 10010.
Manufactured in the United States of America
Library of Congress Catalog Card Number: 77-16749

Library of Congress Cataloging in Publication Data

Schultz, Duane P.
    Wake Island, the hopeless gallant fight.

    Bibliography: p.
    Includes index.
    1. Wake Island, Battle of, 1941-
D767.99.W3S37   940.54'26   77-16749

ISBN 0-312-85451-X

St. Martin's Press, Inc., 175 Fifth Ave., New York, N.Y. 10010

Schultz, Duane P

Contents

Acknowledgments

Many people have given generously of their time during the preparation of this book, and it is no exaggeration to say that it could not have been done without their help.

To the many survivors of Wake who graciously responded to my letters—including Generals Putnam, Potter, and Bayler—I am most appreciative. They all supplied anecdotes and leads to follow up, resolved details not clear in the records, and provided me with exciting living links with history. I have read their letters many times, not only for specific information, but also for the charm and humor with which they described their past and present lives.

I want especially to thank General Devereux for his hospitality in allowing us to visit him at his lovely farm, Wexford, in the Maryland countryside. It was a marvelous experience, and we shall always remember the general's graciousness and patience in probing his files and his memory of those sixteen days on Wake.

I am indebted to Admiral Cunningham for his correspondence and his generosity in supplying me with a great many personal papers.

The papers of Admiral Cunningham and General Devereux are on file with the special collections division of the Mugar Memorial Library at Boston University, and I thank Dr. Howard B. Gotlieb, the director, for his assistance.

I am grateful to Leonn D. Boone of Otsego, Michigan, a longtime student of the battle for Wake Island, whose telephone call "out of the blue" put me in touch with the Wake Island survivors' association. His enthusiasm and insights were of great help. Also, he instigated the drive for formal recognition of Admiral Cunningham's leadership on Wake through the office of the Honorable Garry Brown, United States Representative from Michigan, assisted by Michael E. Brunner.

For the student of World War II, there could be no more interesting place to live than Washington, D.C., for here in the archives of the armed services are millions of documents and reports on every battle and campaign of that conflict. The Historical Center of the United States Marine Corps and the Historical Center of the United States Navy allowed me to examine their holdings on Wake Island and the aborted relief attempt. I wish to thank Lieutenant Colonel R. B. Tiffany, Joyce Bonnett, Ralph Donnelly, Morris Perry, and Henry Shaw of the Marine Corps, Ms. Morgan, the Marine Corps' Historical Branch librarian, and Rita Hallé and Nina Statum of the Navy. Benis M. Frank, head of the Marine Corps' Oral History Program, provided transcriptions of interviews with prominent retired Marine Corps officers. Master Sergeant Ashley and George Craig of the Marine Corps' Photo Archives, and the staff of the Still Picture Branch of the National Archives, were extremely helpful in selecting photographs for the book. These people are all dedicated and knowledgeable; a researcher could not ask for greater cooperation.

Wide World Photos, Inc., supplied the photograph of the Wake Island prisoners aboard ship. Two United States Marine Corps historical monographs (R. D. Heinl's *The Defense of Wake* and F. O. Hough's *Pearl Harbor to Guadalcanal*) provided the basis for the maps.

Ann Whyte of Pan American World Airways provided a wealth of material about the Pan Am facilities on Wake and other fascinating insights into those pioneering and glamorous days of early transoceanic flight. The establishment of air service between America and Asia in

1935 is a story of great courage, initiative, and daring on the part of Pan Am.

The National Air and Space Museum of the Smithsonian Institution permitted me to be photographed with the Wildcat in the Sea–Air Operations room. My thanks to Lynne Murphy, Louise Hull, and Tim Wooldridge of the museum, and to my photographer, Jack Mervis.

At St. Martin's Press, Tom Dunne proved a most helpful and enthusiastic editor, and Denis Holler smoothly handled the many production details.

The diligent research and editorial work of my wife, Sydney Ellen, was vital in transforming the idea of a book into printed pages.

I hope that all of those who helped will be pleased with what I have tried to make of their efforts.

Duane Schultz

1

"So Far, The News Has All Been Bad"

Air raid sirens are wailing in San Francisco. The army reports a flight of thirty Japanese airplanes over the city, heading inland. People living along the coast of Oregon and Washington expect an invasion fleet off their shore at any moment. Up and down the Pacific coast and as far inland as Boise, Idaho, cities are blacked out. Crowds gather on street corners and yell at motorists who are driving with their lights on.

The Pacific Telephone and Telegraph Company building in San Francisco is barricaded with sandbags. Some thousand homes around Monterey and Carmel are evacuated. It is decided to move the Rose Bowl game—for New Year's Day, 1942—to the Duke University stadium in North Carolina. The winter racing season at Santa Anita is canceled.

In Washington, D.C., the War Department is just as jittery and unsure as the average citizen. Excited officers cluster in the corridors and speculate on where the next attack will come. "Anywhere" is the answer; no one knows where the enemy fleet that attacked Pearl Harbor is. The locks of the Panama Canal could be the next target, or the aircraft factories in California. A high government official, in a state of hysteria, telephones the White House to demand that the entire West Coast be abandoned and a defense line set up in the Rocky Mountains.

It is Tuesday night, the ninth of December, 1941. Millions of Americans sit glum and tight-lipped around their radio sets to hear the familiar voice of President Franklin Delano Roosevelt as he confirms their worst fears. It was just a little more than forty-eight hours ago that they were jolted into war.

"So far, the news has all been bad," Roosevelt says.

Rumors, confusion, uncertainty, and anger have gripped the nation. The lines at the recruiting offices have been blocks long during the day. Many of them are remaining open tonight to handle the surge of volunteers. Some young men got in line before dawn to be the first to enlist—to fight back, to take revenge.

"We have suffered a serious setback in Hawaii," Roosevelt continues.

No one knows with any certainty, not even the president himself, how serious things are—only that the situation is bad and likely to get worse. Where will the Japs strike next?

At Pearl Harbor in the Hawaiian Islands, the military forces brace themselves as best they can with what is left for another attack. They expect not just a bombing raid, but a full-scale invasion of Oahu or one of the other islands.

Reports are coming in from Wake Island; it is being bombed. A dispatch from the Reuters News Agency out of Shanghai says that Wake has already been occupied by the Japanese. Why would the enemy want Wake? The generals and admirals know—the enemy expects to use it as a springboard for attacks on Midway and Hawaii. In his broadcast, Roosevelt says solemnly that the news from Wake is confused, "but we must be prepared for the announcement that [it has been] seized."

The attack on Pearl Harbor is the most humiliating and overwhelming military defeat the United States has ever suffered. The entire Pacific Fleet has been wiped out, or so it is thought at the time. In the "little Pearl Harbor" attack in the Philippines a day later, MacArthur's air force is almost totally destroyed on the ground; only a few planes remain.

Everywhere in the Pacific in the days and weeks ahead, America and her new allies, the British and the Dutch, will reel from one lightning blow after another. Everywhere there will be losses and retreats and defeats, one humiliation after another. Disasters and surrenders will become daily occurrences, except on one tiny, lonely, isolated island that few people have ever heard of. The early reports are wrong; Wake Island has not been taken. It is holding its own. The marines are fighting back! For sixteen days following Pearl Harbor it will be bombed every day but one, and still the marines will hold.

"Marines Keep Wake" reports the *New York Times* on December 12. Wake Island becomes a watchword, a symbol, a heroic stand on the part of a handful of the glamorous leathernecks. Their courage eases some of the hurt and shame of Pearl Harbor. The *Washington Post* says that Wake Island has become "the stage for an epic in American military history, one of those gallant stands such as led Texans 105 years ago to cry 'Remember the Alamo!' "

"Wake Up!" becomes a national slogan.* Newspapers trumpet the story of the siege of Wake on the front page of edition after edition. And then, on December 11, an incredible event—the small garrison fights off an

---

* The slogan originated in the Press Room of the State Department and was accompanied by the thumbs-up victory salute.

invasion attempt, sinks two enemy ships, and damages others. These are the first Japanese ships sunk by American forces.

It is America's first victory, the first small step on what everyone knows will be a long and painful road back. Americans stand a little taller that day and swell with pride at the cockiness of the marines. A new phrase enters the consciousness of the nation. When the garrison is asked if it needs anything, the reply is, "Send us more Japs!" This quickly becomes a rallying cry, a gallant, flippant message that captures and reflects America's determination to fight back and win. Of course, it was never really said, but that didn't come out until after the war, and then it wasn't needed any longer.

At a press conference on December 13, President Roosevelt echoes the pride of 130 million Americans as he pays tribute to the marines of Wake. Yet he tempers his words with a note of caution. He knows Wake may not be able to hold out much longer. The public should be prepared for the possibility of another defeat. Hopes must not be allowed to rise too high. On the same day, the *New York Times* says in an editorial: "They have held the fort and kept Old Glory flying. . . . They may yet be annihilated. . . . But they have fought gallantly, and by their gallantry they have carried on in the finest tradition of their corps."

And still they continue to hold. Casualties mount, defenses are shattered, and Japanese bombers return day after day. In great secrecy, a task force is assembled amidst the ruins of Pearl Harbor. Troops and supplies are loaded aboard ship, and the small fleet glides out into the unknown waters of the Pacific on a course that will take them 2,000 miles westward. "We're headed for Wake!" the marines shout. The island's defenders are told they can expect reinforcements.

The attrition continues while the ships move cautiously closer and closer. Then, 425 miles from Wake—

less than a day's sailing time—they turn away and head back to Pearl Harbor. On the aircraft carrier *Saratoga*, marine pilots curse their leaders; some break down in tears. The lives of fellow marines are at stake. On the bridge of the flagship, officers urge Admiral Frank Jack Fletcher to disobey his orders and continue on to Wake. Angry words are exchanged. Some consider the situation close to mutiny. An admiral walks off the bridge in bitterness.

And from Wake comes the message: "Enemy on island—issue in doubt." But there is no doubt. There can be no beating back this new invasion, not without reinforcements. The marines are too few and too tired and too poorly equipped.

2

"To Deny Wake to The Enemy"

It takes only a brief glimpse at a 1941 map of the Pacific to see why Wake Island was considered to be of such strategic value to the United States and why it was such an early target in Japan's program of conquest. As the war planners on both sides saw the situation in the late 1930s, possession of Wake was vital to the defense of their territory.

To the Japanese, it was a potentially deadly dagger, thrust into the heart of their mid-Pacific possessions. If the Americans fortified it and built an air base, some of Japan's most important outposts would be within the range of heavy bombers. Wake was perilously close to the boundary line of the Japanese mandate. The Marshall Islands were barely 600 miles due south, the Japanese base at Taongi only 425 miles away. The most important of Japan's air bases in the Kwajalein Atoll were only 620 miles distant. Of all the American bases in the mid-Pacific, Wake was closest to the Japanese homeland itself. With the exception of Guam, it was the greatest threat to vital Japanese naval and air bases in the Pacific.

Japanese planners agreed that in the coming war between the two countries Wake would have to be taken in the first few days of hostilities. In their timetable, Wake (along with Guam and Midway) was scheduled for early occupation. Hawaii must be America's westernmost point of intrusion into what was to become a Japanese sea. Accordingly a special force—the Fourth Fleet under the command of Vice Admiral Nariyoshi Inouye—was established. It was an amphibious force with troops specially trained in the art of assaulting beaches, and it was headquartered in the giant harbor at Truk in the Caroline Islands.

Admiral Inouye's mission had been planned as early as 1938, when the fundamental East Asia war plan was formulated. By November 1941, navy and army commanders were given more detailed instructions. Inouye's orders in reference to Wake were simple: capture it! The Japanese knew how lightly Wake was defended, and so it seemed a direct and easy mission to accomplish. So certain were Japanese planners that Wake would be nothing more than a small operation that they assigned a landing force of only 450 men. It was a decision they would regret.

American planners had also been busy preparing for war in the Pacific, a war some military leaders had been predicting since the 1920s. The question was not "Will there be a war?" or "Who will be the enemy?" but "When will it come?" Throughout the 1930s, a series of contingency plans, the so-called color plans, were devised with a different color assigned to each potential enemy. Japan's color was orange.*

With the outbreak of war in Europe and the formation of the Axis coalition, this planning was modified in

---

* Yellow was the original choice for the war plan against the Japanese, but it was dropped for fear that the Japanese would know immediately that yellow referred to them.

the direction of a truly worldwide war involving more than one enemy. Combining the individual colors of the previous plans, the military developed the "Rainbow" plan. As the world situation continued to darken, newer versions evolved until, in 1941, Rainbow 5 constituted the basic American strategy for winning the war in the Pacific.

It was an optimistic scenario which totally ignored the warnings of people like General Billy Mitchell and others who predicted that the war would begin with a sneak attack on Pearl Harbor on a peaceful Sunday morning.* Rainbow 5 was based on the full availability of the Pacific Fleet. Behind a spearhead of battleships, American forces would move westward from their base in Hawaii when war was declared and capture all the islands of the Marshall, Gilbert, and Caroline chains and thus be able to reinforce the Philippines. This was to take no more than six months.

In addition, Rainbow 5 called for an advance screen of fortifications west of the main base at Pearl Harbor. Like a line of cavalry forts in the Old West, these island bastions were to be a first line of defense, keeping the enemy far from Hawaii. With roving patrol planes constantly in motion for miles around each island, the presence of any enemy fleet would be easily detected. Bombers and fighters could take off from these outposts to harass any ships trying to get through the "wall" and could also bomb Japanese islands. These outposts were to form a protective barrier, sealing off Hawaii and the West Coast of the United States. There were to be five

---

* In 1921, Major Earl H. Ellis. USMC, wrote a report, "Advance Base Operations in Micronesia," predicting a Japanese air attack on Pearl Harbor in the early hours of a Sunday morning. General Hugh Drum, former commander of army forces in Hawaii, offered a similar prediction in 1936. General Frederick Martin and Admiral Pat Bellinger, commanders of army and navy air forces in Hawaii at the time of Pearl Harbor, also warned of a dawn attack.

of these advance island bases: Johnston, Palmyra, Samoa, Midway, and Wake. Wake would be the most important because it was the closest to Japanese territory.

Wake stood far out in front of the line drawn from north to south through the other islands. Only Guam was in a more exposed position. In the center of the Marianas, Guam was ringed on all sides by the Japanese and therefore was written off in the American war plan. There was nothing its 153 Marines could do; their capture was a footnote in Rainbow 5.*

It was a detailed plan thick with maps, analyses, movements of forces, and timetables. The island fortresses were to be both a line of defense and a springboard for attack. There was only one thing wrong with this island outpost concept. When war began, their defenses were not ready.

In 1938, a board of naval officers led by Rear Admiral A. J. Hepburn recommended that $7,500,000 be allocated to develop Wake as an air base. Congress provided the funds, but not for two years, and it was yet another year before work actually began. The first civilian work party reached the island in January 1941—eleven months before Pearl Harbor—to begin the three-year construction program. It was not until August 1941 that the first detachment of marines arrived, and only four days before the war began that a squadron of outdated fighter planes landed. It was the old story—too little, too obsolete, too late.

Thus, tiny Wake Island assumed a role of major importance in the preparations for war on both sides, an importance thrust upon it by an accident of location. There was nothing else of value about the island. For

---

* Earlier plans had called for extensive fortifications of Guam, but on February 23, 1939, Congress voted against any such development for fear of provoking the Japanese.

more than 350 years since its discovery it had remained unknown and unwanted, a dot on the map rising at its highest point only twenty-one feet above the level of the sea around it. Yet soon men would die for that barren spot.

Wake Island was first sighted in 1586 by a Spanish explorer, Alvaro de Mendana, whose two ships were running low on food and water. Coming ashore, he found to his disgust only brambles, sand, and coral. He named it San Francisco and sailed away.

In 1796 it was discovered again, this time by Samuel Wake, captain of the *Prince William Henry,* an English trading ship. Captain Wake fixed its latitude and longitude precisely and gave it his name. Not long after, the island was discovered a third time by another British ship, the *Halcyon,* whose captain was unaware of Captain Wake's earlier visit.

The first American ship to visit Wake was the U.S.S. *Vincennes,* which arrived on December 20, 1840. One of the passengers, a well-known explorer named Charles Wilkes, surveyed the atoll and gave his name to one of the islands. With him was a naturalist, Titian Peale, who collected species of marine life and named the third island in the atoll after himself. There were no more islands to name after that.

Wake remained in isolation until the stormy night of March 5, 1866, when the *Libelle,* a German ship en route from Honolulu to Hong Kong, foundered on a reef offshore. For three days passengers and crew clung to the ship as it slowly broke to pieces. Then, when the storm finally subsided, they were able to get ashore with $300,000 that was part of the cargo. They found themselves shipwrecked on an island that offered no food or water and was far from the main shipping lanes. For three weeks they lived on what they had salvaged from the ship and worked frantically to recondition two small boats from the *Libelle* that had somehow survived the storm. They hid the money on the island and set sail for Guam, some 1,400 miles away. The largest boat, twenty-two feet long, reached Guam eighteen days later. One of its passengers was a noted opera singer, Mme. Anna Bishop, who reportedly sang to her fellow passengers most of the time to keep up their morale. The other boat, with the *Libelle's* captain and seven other people aboard, was never seen again. The money was recovered soon after by a ship sent out from Guam. As recently as 1940, parts of the *Libelle*, including the anchor, could be found on Wake.

The atoll fell back into obscurity for another thirty years until the Spanish-American War. The fleet carrying American troops to the Philippines stopped at Wake on July 4, 1898. The commander, Major General Francis V. Greene, came ashore and raised a small American flag which was tied to a dead limb. Another American ship came to Wake in the following year to formally take possession of the atoll in the name of the United States. The reason Washington wanted it was to establish a cable station, but that idea was quickly dropped when it was learned that there was no fresh water available. The cable, like the rest of history, went past Wake without stopping.

There were occasional brief stopovers in the next two decades. In 1906 a young American army captain, John J. Pershing, came ashore and put up a more durable canvas flag. From time to time, Japanese fishermen stopped to look for fresh water, and in 1922 and 1923 American surveying and scientific expeditions landed. In the 1930s, Wake was essentially no different than when it had first been discovered. Except for some flotsam from the wrecked German ship, the atoll had not changed in over three centuries.

Finally, in 1935, a group of men stepped ashore to build and to stay. What brought about their arrival was not a military or political consideration, but a strictly commercial one.

The airplane changed Wake Island. Pan American Airways embarked on an aggressive program to circle the globe, to carry passengers from the United States across both oceans to the rest of the world. Using large, comfortable four-engine flying boats, the "Clippers," Pan American linked the Far East capitals of Tokyo and Manila to San Francisco. But they needed bases for refueling, protected lagoons where a plane could land and take off safely and where passengers could rest while the aircraft was being serviced. Wake provided a perfect stopping point on the Philippine run, and so, in 1935, construction on a seaplane base began.

The U.S. Navy, recognizing the potential military value of such a base, cooperated with Pan American by undertaking an up-to-date survey of the atoll. Then, in May of 1935, a hundred freightcar loads of men and supplies were landed from a Pan Am construction ship and the transformation of Wake was under way.

It was difficult, backbreaking work, with no relief from the monotony of sun, sand, and sea, but gradually the shape of civilization appeared on Wake Island. A comfortable forty-five-room hotel, the Pan American Airways Inn, was built, a few farm animals imported, vegetables planted, and a small garden laid out with the anchor of the wrecked ship *Libelle* in the center. After only three months, the first Pan Am Clipper landed in the lagoon. Another link in round-the-world air travel had been established.

A Pan Am passenger who might have wanted to go sightseeing on his stopover in 1935 would have found little to interest him, unless he fancied strange rats and little-known species of birds, for they were the only other inhabitants of the atoll. To many people, the rats were the only memorable sight they carried away from

Wake Island. In fact, they became something of a tourist attraction. A pamphlet given to Clipper passengers, entitled *Welcome to Wake*, noted that "amusement may be found in the famous Wakonian hunting expeditions concentrating on the running down of our famous rats. Only the most intrepid should indulge in this sport. Air rifles, and ammunition, can be obtained at the Airport Office."

No one knows how or when rats came to Wake, but they flourished and at times threatened to overrun the island. They had front legs much shorter than their hind legs, and this gave them a curious humpbacked appearance. They were not afraid of people. Many a marine would later wake up in a foxhole to find one crawling over his face. The rats swarmed by the hundreds across the coral and sand, and in and out of buildings. Pan Am employees, and later the marines and civilian construction workers, tried hard to keep them in check, but they craftily ignored the poisoned grain that had been scattered all over the island. The flower beds in the Pan Am compound were their favorite targets, and not even live electric wires could keep them away from such tantalizing food.

If the rats didn't send the 1935 Clipper passenger back to the hotel and he wandered down to the beach, he saw another strange sight—thousands of hermit crabs. There were so many crabs scurrying frantically in tightly packed formations that at times it looked as though the whole beach was moving.

Wake also offered hundreds of birds, strange species adapted to their harsh environment. There was one kind the marines called the "peewee," a red-eyed bird no larger than a robin. What made it unusual was that it could not fly. It was a small puff of feathers without wings or tail. The bosun bird was a large, raucous creature twice the size of a pigeon. It had blood red feet and beak, and bright tail feathers as much as twenty inches long. Somehow it was able to fly backwards. If the visitor looked out to sea, he could watch the pirate birds swoop down on smaller birds and capture their food. The pirate birds had an unfortunate habit of flying in groups in perfect formation at a height where they were later mistaken for airplanes.

There were a great many varieties of fish in the lagoon and among the outer reefs, and fishing equipment was provided for passengers, along with a warning notice. "Large morays may be encountered but it is recommended that these be cut loose as they will be most troublesome if brought ashore. The smaller, white eel should be avoided as they will attack an individual if they are cornered. . . . Shark are in abundance and will provide much thrill."

Coral formations in all conceivable shapes and colors covered the islands, littering the beaches so heavily that walking barefoot was not advised. There were large coral boulders too; one, the size of a large truck, became popular when the bombing started.

Pan American passengers were surprised, as they wandered around, at the absence of palm trees. It seemed somehow unfair to be on a Pacific island that didn't have tall palms waving in the trade winds. Wake's vegetation was a dense undergrowth of shrubs and stunted trees which grew no taller than ten to twenty feet. It was a thick scrub; in many places it was so junglelike that it completely blotted out the sight of the sea.

The stopover passenger in 1935 could actually visit only one of the three islands that make up the atoll. The Pan Am base was located on Peale Island, and there was as yet no bridge connecting it to the larger island of Wake. If he stood on the pier at the seaplane landing and looked across the lagoon, he could see both Wake and Wilkes islands, but there was nothing to visit there but more scrub, sand, and coral.

The passengers had seen the atoll from the air when the giant Clipper came in to land—a U-shaped trio of islands opening to the northwest, toward Japan. The atoll is a submerged volcano top comprising less than four square miles of land area, over half of which is Wake Island. The total distance from Toki Point on Peale Island to Peacock Point on Wake Island to Kuku Point on Wilkes Island is only ten miles. The entire atoll is ringed by a reef very close to the shore, and the lagoon is full of vicious coral heads. The restless Pacific constantly beats against the reef and splashes up on the coral-strewn beaches, causing a continuous roar. The noise never stops, and the marines found to their dismay that it was loud enough to drown out the sound of approaching planes.

There is only one entrance to the lagoon, a shallow channel no more than fifty yards wide. When the wind is strong, it blows water out of the lagoon through the narrow opening like boiling water bubbling out of a small-necked bottle. Beyond the reef, the ocean floor drops down so deep that ships cannot drop anchor.

When ships came to Wake Island to deliver supplies, they had to keep their position in the open water by constantly turning over their engines. Supplies were carefully and laboriously loaded into lighters which were hauled through the channel by heavy tractors on the island. It often took up to ten days to unload a ship.

Fortunately, Pan American passengers never had to remain on Wake for more than an overnight visit. The airline's employees did their best to make them comfortable, but they were always glad to reboard the plane. Then the pilot would taxi cautiously away from the dock, line up on the dredged channel across the lagoon, and push the throttles forward. Gracefully the plane's hull would break free of the surface of the water and rise gently over the southern side of Wake Island on the other side of the lagoon. The passengers would settle

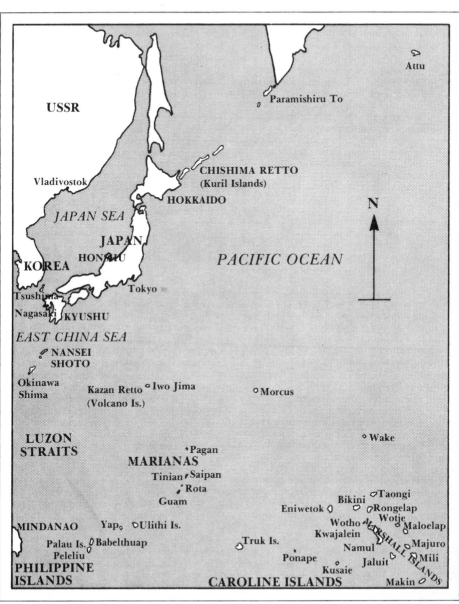

The Pacific Ocean: Japanese Possessions Prior to December 7, 1941

back in their roomy seats for the 1,200-mile flight to Midway, the next stop on their voyage to Honolulu.

On Peale Island, the Pan Am employees resumed their routine and awaited the next flight. There were only two a week, one going east and one going west.

That quiet routine lasted for five years, until January 1941, when the construction finally began which would turn Wake Island into a military base. A contract was awarded to the Contractors Pacific Naval Air Bases organization to build an airfield and facilities for seaplanes. Throughout the Christmas season of 1940, stevedores worked long hours at Pier 31-A in Honolulu to load 2,000 tons of equipment onto the U.S.S. *William Ward Burrows,* which formerly had been 'the *Santa Rita* belonging to the Grace Shipping Line.

The *Burrows,* called by its crew the *Weary Willie* or the *Dierdorff Maru* (in honor of its skipper, Captain Ross Dierdorff), was also taking a construction crew of eighty men to Wake. They were a hardworking, hard-drinking lot, veterans of Boulder and Grand Coulee dams and a score of other big construction projects. Their boss, the construction superintendent for the project, was Dan Teters, a former University of Washington football star and an army sergeant in World War I. He would soon earn the gratitude of every marine on Wake Island.*

An enormous variety of equipment and supplies was crammed into the four cargo hatches of the *Burrows:* trucks and tractors, giant road scrapers and rollers, cement mixers, generators, stoves, refrigerators, water dis-

---

* In a letter to me, Admiral Cunningham described Teters as a "tough guy," ready to use his fists and contemptuous of military brass, at least before the war began. He was "articulate with an Irish ability to express himself well, and to charm and attract others, even including truculent Japanese soldiers." After the war, Teters worked in China, Manila, and North Africa. He died of cancer in 1960.

tillation plants, lumber, steel, dynamite, gasoline, oil, food, cigarettes, chewing gum, and candy.

When the holds were full, the stevedores piled equipment across the cargo hatch covers: diesel oil drums, a thirty-six-foot motor sampan, large cold storage boxes—each with its own refrigerating unit—and two huge steel pontoons. The ship was full, inside and out, but there was still more equipment to take.

A wooden barge, forty feet wide and one hundred feet long, was attached to the towline of the *Burrows*. Called *Wake No. 1*, it was loaded with an eighty-ton diesel crane, two bulldozers, a tractor, and two six-thousand-pound anchors. In addition, a fifty-five foot tug, the *Pioneer*, accompanied the *Burrows*, carrying an icebox, water-breakers, and a life raft.

On the day after Christmas the construction crew, known as the Pioneer Party, came aboard the *Burrows*. They wore leis around their necks and some of them had hangovers. On the dock, a small group of wives and girlfriends waved and cried as the *Burrows* with its barge and tug pulled away. It was a difficult voyage—the barge twice broke loose—and they reached Wake on January 8, 1941. Then began the tiring job of getting all the equipment ashore.

Work progressed at a feverish pace. Runways, roads, the dredged channel, workshops, living quarters—all began to take shape. Aside from the biweekly arrival of the Clippers, the only diversion was the occasional appearance of a Japanese airplane ominously keeping track of the construction.

At Pearl Harbor, Admiral Husband E. Kimmel, commander in chief of the Pacific Fleet (who would be forced to resign as a result of the Japanese attack), was growing increasingly concerned about Wake. He knew that in spite of its recognized importance, it was still totally defenseless. Something would have to be done.

On April 18, 1941, Kimmel expressed his concern in a letter to his superior, Admiral Harold R. Stark, chief of naval operations, in Washington, D.C.

"The strategic importance of Wake is increasingly evident, as one inquires into the means by which the Pacific Fleet may carry on offensive operations to the westward. . . .

"To deny Wake to the enemy, without occupying it ourselves would be difficult; to recapture it if the Japanese should seize it in the early period of hostilities, would require operations of some magnitude. Since the Japanese Fourth Fleet (based in the mandated islands) includes transports and troops with equipment especially suited for landing operations, it appears not unlikely that one of the initial operations of the Japanese may be directed against Wake.

"If Wake be defended, then for the Japanese to reduce it would require extended operations of their naval forces in an area where we might be able to get at them; thus affording us opportunity to get at naval forces with naval forces. We should try, by every possible means, to get the Japanese to expose naval units. In order to do this, we must provide objectives that require such exposure."

Kimmel urged that a large force of marines be sent to Wake no later than June 1. On June 23, Admiral Stark ordered elements of the First Defense Battalion, Fleet Marine Force, sent to Wake "as soon as practicable." That turned out to be almost two months later. On August 8, the U.S.S. *Regulus,* a twenty-year-old transport, left Honolulu with five officers and 173 enlisted men. They arrived at Wake on August 19. Defensive preparations had finally begun.

At the same time, about 2,500 miles to the northwest, a different kind of preparation was under way. At airfields on Kyushu, the southernmost island of Japan, pilots were practicing dive-bombing and low-level torpedo runs over terrain carefully chosen to duplicate that surrounding Pearl Harbor.

A week later, on September 2, a meeting was held at the Naval War College in a suburb of Tokyo. Present were some forty of the highest ranking officers in Japan's army and navy. Tabletop maneuvers were conducted and then analyzed and criticized. The final details of the simultaneous attacks against Pearl Harbor, Malaya, the Philippines, the Dutch East Indies, and the islands of the central Pacific were worked out. Far down on the list of targets was one of the smallest and therefore presumably easiest to take—Wake Island.

3

"Do The Best You Can"

In Chevy Chase, Maryland, a pleasant tree-lined suburb north of Washington, D.C., a major with the United States Marine Corps was enjoying the first day of his leave with his wife and seven-year-old son. It was colder there than at his station in San Diego, California, and he was tired from the long cross-country journey, but that didn't bother him. It had been a long time since he had been home, and he was prepared to relax, see a lot of old friends, and marvel at how fast his son Paddy was growing.

It was January 1941, and he was grateful for this short break in the feverish training activities as the marines readied themselves for war.

The doorbell rang. It was Western Union with a telegram ordering him back to his post immediately. He packed his bag and said good-bye to his family. He would never see his wife again; it would be four years before he would see his son.

His brother drove him to the train at Union Station, a few blocks from the Capitol.

"What's it mean?" he asked. "Are you going to be transferred somewhere else?"

The major shook his head and sighed.

"Oh, I'll probably wind up on some little spit-kit of an island."

They talked on, of family and old times, but the conversation kept returning to the international situation and the threat of war with Japan.

"What do you think will happen?" his brother asked.

"Your guess is as good as mine," the major replied, "but I'll probably wind up eating fish and rice."

It was not a pleasant prediction, but it was an accurate one.

The brothers shook hands, and Major James Patrick Sinnot Devereux, USMC, pulled himself aboard the coach and started the long, tedious trip west, a trip that would take him to Wake Island and then to a prisoner-of-war camp in Japanese-occupied China.

Not quite a year later, his picture would be splashed on the front pages of newspapers all across the country as the "hero of Wake Island," and his name would become a household word along with Colin Kelley, Jonathan Wainwright, and other formerly obscure military men who devoted their careers to the war that was looming on the horizon.

Devereux was thirty-eight years old, a thin, wiry, five-foot-five inch veteran of eighteen years in the Marine Corps. Son of an army medical officer, Devereux was born in Cuba in 1903 and educated in Maryland, Washington, D.C., and Lausanne, Switzerland. He enlisted in the Marine Corps in 1923 and was commissioned a second lieutenant two years later.* He had served in Nicaragua, China, Pearl Harbor, and the Philippines, as well as in the United States, and had been awarded the Second Nicaraguan Campaign Medal, Yangtze Service Medal, and the Marine Corps Expeditionary Medal for China. While stationed in China

---

* In my interview with General Devereux, he joked that he joined the Marine Corps because he "liked the red stripe on the marine trousers!"

at the American Legation at Peiping, he married Mary Walsh, daughter of an army colonel.

Devereux liked his work, did it very well, and was highly thought of by his men and his superiors. He had a reputation for great thoroughness in preparation and planning. A fellow officer once said of him, "He's the kind of guy who would put all the mechanized aircraft detectors into operation and then station a man with a spyglass in a tall tree."

When he arrived in San Diego, Devereux received orders to report to Pearl Harbor as executive officer of the First Defense Battalion under the command of Lieutenant Colonel Bertram Bone. The defense battalion concept was a new idea in the corps, established in 1939. Its purpose was to defend small islands of the kind now being hastily prepared for war. Ideally such a battalion included 43 officers and 909 men, with heavy weapons for use against both airplanes and ships. The battalion consisted of a coastal defense group (five-inch naval guns), an antiaircraft group (three-inch guns), a machine gun group for beach defense (.50 and .30 caliber), a searchlight battery, and various headquarters and service functions. There was no infantry component as such because all marines were trained to perform as infantrymen in addition to whatever technical specialty they had. However, since most of the men were assigned to heavy weapons, there was no reserve force left to deal with enemy troops should they successfully land on a beach.

But, in accordance with the defense battalion concept, that wasn't supposed to happen, as Devereux found out before he left for Wake. He talked at some length with two of his superior officers—Col. Harry Pickett, assistant operations officer on Admiral Kimmel's staff, and Lieutenant Colonel Omar T. Pfeiffer, whose job was to coordinate the defense units sent to the various islands. Both men made clear to Devereux the nature of his mission; it was not expected that the marines would be able to hold out against a full-fledged invasion attempt. Their job was to defend the island against minor attacks of the type made by German raiders against certain British Pacific islands during World War I. Several times during that period, a single German ship shelled an island and then sent a small landing party ashore to destroy radio facilities and capture supplies. Wake and the other island outposts had to be strong enough, as soon as possible, to resist such hit-and-run attacks. In time they would be able to resist heavier raids, once the defensive preparations were complete.

"And what do we do in the case of a full-scale attack?" Devereux asked.

"Do the best you can."

On October 15, 1941, Major Devereux arrived on Wake Island aboard the U.S.S. *Regulus,* bringing with him the heavy firepower around which the defense of Wake would be built. These weapons, which Devereux's men were to use to such telling advantage, included six five-inch .51 caliber guns taken from World War I battleships, twelve three-inch guns (only one of which had full fire-control equipment), eighteen .50 caliber machine guns, and thirty .30 caliber machine guns.

When he stepped ashore, Devereux found a frenzied pace of construction under way. The civilian work force had been increased to 1,146 men, and they were scattered all over the three islands bulldozing, dynamiting, dredging, and building. A 1935 Pan American Clipper passenger returning to Wake during the fall of 1941 would not have recognized the place.

There were now, in addition to the Pan Am facility on Peale Island, two large camps on the extreme ends of Wake Island facing each other across the lagoon. Camp 1, close to the channel between Wake and Wilkes, once the home of the construction workers, was now a marine camp. While barracks and officers' quarters were being built, the marines lived and ate in neat rows of tents stretched over wooden frames. They were comfortable enough, with wooden decks and open-screened sides to allow the cooling trade winds to flow through.

There was an officers' club in a tent smaller than the others, but it contained the islands' most prized possession—iceboxes filled with cold beer. Camp 1 had its own electric power from generators, mess facilities, and a PX.

It was the civilian camp, however, that was the height of luxury in these primitive surroundings. Camp 2 had more permanent buildings and better food, a hospital, a better stocked commissary, a barbershop, an ice-cream parlor, an outdoor movie theatre, and tennis courts. The workers had blasted a small swimming pool out of the coral-filled lagoon and erected a heavy wire net to keep away sharks and moray eels.

All the facilities at Camp 2 were available to the marines, and now there was a gleaming white road of crushed coral running the full length of Wake from one camp to the other, a distance of seven miles. At the base of the U-shaped Wake Island, the airfield was being constructed. The main runway, 5,000 feet long and 200 feet wide, was almost finished, and the shorter crossing runways were under way. Near the landing strip were five huge magazines and three smaller ones, partly underground, built of reinforced concrete. Living quarters for pilots and crew were going up, along with warehouses and shops. A 25,000-gallon aboveground gasoline storage tank stood near the east end of the runway, and a large number of gasoline drums were stacked at the runway apron.

But there was one important thing lacking at the airfield that proved disastrous to Wake's small air force. There were no protected revetments for the planes. When they arrived, the planes would have to sit out in the open.

Near the northeast tip of Wake, three small but comfortable cottages had been built, residences for Dan Teters and for the ranking officers and guest quarters for VIPs.

Beyond Camp 2, a new causeway linked Wake with Peale Island, where the naval air station, a base for seaplanes, was being built. Barracks and a navy hospital were under construction, and concrete was being shaped into a ramp and apron for the patrol planes to use whenever they might come, to pull up on dry land. Out in the once peaceful lagoon, a dredge was noisily cutting off coral heads to enlarge the seaplane landing area.

Across the lagoon, Wilkes Island remained the least developed. It was separated from Wake by the channel which was being enlarged. Small boats manned by sailors stood ready to ferry passengers across. Plans called for a submarine base, but no work had started on it yet. A single road was in place, along with two aboveground gasoline storage tanks which belonged to Pan American. Construction was due to start shortly on powder magazines, and a new channel was being dug across a narrow part of the island to allow ships to enter the lagoon.

The construction seemed to be going well, but it had first priority, ahead of any installations for defense. So Devereux was forced to put his marines to work with picks and shovels to fashion gun emplacements. Occasionally Dan Teters made a bulldozer available. Plagued by a shortage of men, equipment, and time, the marines worked twelve-hour days to prepare the atoll to defend itself. So urgent was this work that all training activities were suspended despite the fact that some of the men had been in the corps only a few months. It was hot, dirty, tough work, but there was no other way to get it done.

It was a race against time, spurred on by a communique received from Pearl Harbor in early

November. "International situation indicates that you should be on the alert."

In the face of this warning, Devereux wanted to stop all nonessential construction and immediately put all civilians to work on bomb shelters, aircraft revetments, and the vital gun emplacements. The line of authority, however, was clearly drawn between the military and civilian areas of responsibility, and Devereux could not on his own assign the civilians to anything other than what they were contracted to do. In order to speed up the defense preparations, Devereux sent a priority cable to Pearl Harbor.

"Does international situation indicate employment of contractor's men on defense installations which are far from complete?"

Fully confident that, considering the circumstances, he would be allowed to make use of the civilians, Devereux met with Dan Teters and Lieutenant Commander Elmer B. Greey, resident officer-in-charge, the military supervisor of the construction program. Both Greey and Teters were very cooperative and began the job of detailing work crew assignments and shifts of equipment and assigning priorities to the various fortifications. When Pearl Harbor replied two days later, however, the answer was negative. The marines were left to fortify the islands on their own.

In a way, the reply was a relief to Devereux, for it suggested that the international situation was not as ominous as the earlier communiqué had indicated. Were Wake in imminent danger, he thought, Pearl Harbor would have approved his request. He continued to work the men twelve hours a day, seven days a week, but with the feeling that there was a little more time to get the island ready for war than he had thought previously.

On November 2, the U.S.S. *Castor* arrived with 9 officers and 200 men, bringing Wake's strength up to 388 marines.

The following day, in Japan, Admiral Osami Nagano, Chief of the Naval General Staff, approved the plan for the opening of Japan's tide of conquest. Two days later, Admiral Yamamoto issued a 151-page report to his key commanders: "Combined Fleet Top Secret Operation Order No. 1." The clock was set ticking.

In mid-November, a tall, thin naval officer sat drinking coffee in the tiny wardroom of the U.S.S. *Wright*, a navy seaplane tender. Tied to the dock at Ford Island in Pearl Harbor, it rocked gently in the wake of passing ships. After eighteen months as navigator of the *Wright*, Commander Winfield Scott "Spiv" Cunningham was being reassigned, and he was not happy about it. He had hoped for stateside duty but found himself detailed to Johnston Island, "surely the most godforsaken atoll in the Pacific. I had been trying for two weeks to get accustomed to that sad blow."

Then a reprieve appeared in the form of new orders. They were not what he wanted, but they seemed a lot better than what he had. The executive officer of the *Wright*, Commander Dixie Kiefer, came into the wardroom and grinned at him.

"Well, Spiv," he said, "you've been groaning at the thought of duty on Johnston Island. Think you'll like Wake any better?"

He handed Cunningham a dispatch ordering him to Wake for temporary duty as OINC (officer-in-charge) of all naval activities.

Cunningham read the orders, then smiled broadly at Kiefer.

"It beats Johnston," he said. "Wake has trees." He had seen both islands on past trips on the *Wright.*

Another officer sitting nearby chimed in, "Yes, but it's also about fifteen hundred miles closer to Japan. Sure you want to get that close?"

Cunningham laughed. "By Christmas," he said, "you'll

be up to your ears in the fighting and I'll be taking my ease as a prisoner of war in Tokyo, with a geisha girl sitting on my knee."

A graduate of the Naval Academy in 1919, Cunningham had spent most of his career sailing in the waters of the Far East. In 1924, he went through flying school at Pensacola, Florida, followed by a series of assignments from shore duty at San Diego and Pearl Harbor to sea duty aboard the first aircraft carrier, *Langley*, and the soon-to-be-famous carriers, *Lexington* and *Yorktown*. As officer-in-charge at Wake, he would be back in aviation again; after eighteen months on a seaplane tender, it was a welcome relief.

It was pure chance that Cunningham's orders had been changed. Another man had been assigned to Wake, but for some reason he was unable to get there as quickly as his orders called for. Since the post at Wake was considered more urgent than the one at Johnston, Cunningham was switched because he was the nearest qualified officer available. As senior officer on Wake, he would be in overall command of the atoll, a position he was to spend years after his release from a POW camp trying to prove. (And his wife was to spend the early months of his captivity trying to establish that he had even been on Wake, much less in command of it.)

With the new orders in hand, Cunningham went to see Admiral Claude Bloch, commandant of the Fourteenth Naval District, to discuss his assignment. With his fellow officers, Cunningham had often discussed the possibility of war. It had been a common topic of wardroom bull sessions for years. Now, as commander of Wake, the question of war seemed more important to him than ever.

He saw the admiral's chief of staff, Captain J. B. Earle, who stressed that Cunningham's primary mission was to accelerate the construction program. Nothing—not even Wake's defensive fortifications—was to interfere with that, Earle said. Cunningham talked with another superior, Rear Admiral Pat Bellinger, commander of all the patrol plane squadrons in the Pacific. Cunningham brought up the same question: what would Wake's role be in the event of war? But again the talk focused on routine matters. Like Captain Earle, Admiral Bellinger did not discuss the possibility of war, and so Cunningham returned to his ship "feeling that the tour of duty on Wake would be uneventful."

The *Wright* was heavily loaded with more supplies for Wake, including materiel and men to support the marine air squadron that the airfield was being readied to receive. Accompanying Cunningham were Commander Campbell Keene, three ensigns, and thirty sailors whose job was to provide support for the navy flying boats that were to be based on Wake and patrol the surrounding ocean for signs of Japanese activity. Also on board was a USMC communications specialist, Major Walter Bayler, going to Wake to set up ground-to-air radio facilities in advance of the arrival of the planes. With Bayler was the squadron's forty-seven-man ground crew of mechanics and other personnel under the command of Second Lieutenant Robert J. Conderman, who would be among the first to die on Wake.

The *Wright* sailed on the morning of Thursday, November 20, 1941. As was the custom by then, the ship was blacked out at night and life jackets were kept close at hand. It was an uneventful trip, and they spotted the water tower, Wake's tallest structure, on Friday morning, November 28.

Commander Cunningham wrote a note in a Christmas card to his daughter and left it at the mail drop. Having learned in his navy career never to leave personal effects behind, he took with him from the *Wright* his dress blue uniforms, many extra changes of clothes, a shortwave radio (so he could listen to the army-navy game), and his golf clubs.

As the small boat prepared to pull away from the *Wright,* Cunningham looked up at the bridge and saw that the ship's chief quartermaster, with whom he had worked for eighteen months, was shaking his head sadly, "as if he was offering me his condolences. Later I was never able to decide whether he suspected Wake was in for trouble, or whether he was simply thinking it was no spot for a golfer.

"Either way, he was right."

Shortly after his arrival, Cunningham was taken on a tour of the atoll by Major Devereux and his executive officer, Major George H. Potter, Jr. There was much left to be done, but the new island commander was impressed by what had been accomplished, both by the civilian crews and by the marines. "Wake was truly coming to life," he wrote.

The marines had a new and much resented responsibility that took precious time away from their preparation of the islands' defenses. They had to refuel the giant B-17s which were using Wake as a stopover on their long flights from California to the Philippines. The planes had to be refueled and on their way as fast as possible. Sometimes the marines worked all night to accomplish the job. What made the work so hard and tedious was that Wake had no proper facilities for refueling.

Each plane took 3,000 gallons of gas, most of which had to be pumped by hand. They had only one small fuel truck, so gas was transferred from the large storage tanks into 50-gallon drums which were then hauled to the planes and pumped into the fuel tanks. When several planes landed at the same time, refueling could take up to twenty-four hours. Then the empty drums were refilled so as to be ready for the next flight and placed far apart among the brush in case of attack.*

* Most of the B-17s refueled so laboriously on Wake were destroyed on the ground on the first day of the war in the Philippines.

In addition, whenever a ship came to Wake, the marines were pressed into service as stevedores, loading heavy equipment onto the lighters, then unloading it on land and delivering it to its destination on one of the three islands.

Before Cunningham arrived to replace him as island commander, Devereux also had to spend time greeting VIPs who passed through on the Clippers. Generals and admirals, important foreign and American diplomats, noted correspondents—all had to be welcomed at the dock and given as much of the red-carpet treatment as Wake could provide. One flight brought Saburo Kurusu, a high-ranking Japanese diplomat on his way to Washington for a last-minute peace effort (in ignorance of the plans to attack Pearl Harbor). Kurusu walked up the ramp from the plane and nodded at Devereux's greeting.

"I suppose you have come to tell me that I can't leave the hotel?" Kurusu said.

"No sir," Devereux replied, "but you know how these things are. None of the passengers may leave the vicinity of the hotel without special permission."

The two men went into the lobby of the Pan American hotel, sat down, and ordered drinks—scotch and soda for Kurusu.

"I became accustomed to it in the Philippines many years ago," he said.

Devereux was impressed with Kurusu's perfect English, refined, no doubt, by the diplomat's American wife of some years. They talked for more than an hour, ordering several rounds of drinks, and Kurusu paid for each one.

"I have ample funds to take care of things like that."

They spoke of many things but cautiously skirted the issue of war between their two countries.

"I am just going to Washington to see what I can do,"

Kurusu said. "I hope I can straighten out affairs and avoid trouble."

Despite these constant interruptions, Devereux and his men were able to make good progress in fortifying the atoll. The coastal defense weapons, antiaircraft weapons, and beach defense machine guns were in place at strategic points on the three islands.

The heavy five-inch guns were concentrated at the three extremes of the atoll, batteries of two each at Peacock, Toki, and Kuku points. They were permanently emplaced and could be used only against surface targets, not aircraft. Devereux had done a magnificent job of placement and camouflage of these weapons.

From as close as a hundred yards offshore they could not be seen, so skillfully were they blended in with their surroundings. The base or mount of each gun was buried, and the rest surrounded by sandbags painted the same colors as the background. The guns themselves were painted in random designs of green, buff, and black. Branches were stuck in the coral around each gun, and the leaves painted to blend in with real trees. Camouflage netting secured by large rocks covered the whole area. Major Bayler, on first seeing the emplacements at Peacock Point, commented that "the general appearance of the entire locality was that of an innocent thicket." Shelters for the gun crews had not yet been built, but the weapons were ready for use.

Three batteries (each with four guns) of the three-inch antiaircraft weapons were set up in the general vicinity of the heavier weapons. These pieces were not permanently in place, but they could be moved only with difficulty, as the marines would later find out. Some, but not all, of the antiaircraft guns were protected by sandbags, and only some had adequate shelters for crews and ammunition.

At various points along the beaches, in some cases

very close to the water, the .50 and .30 caliber machine guns were set up in dugouts. The only other weapons were rifles, a few submachine guns, and pistols, kept in readiness in the tents. The naval personnel and the four-man army communications team headed by Captain Henry S. Wilson were unarmed; they did not even have helmets. Six searchlights were placed at various points along the beach, each with its generator sunk into a pit.

The concentration of heavy weapons and their fields of fire, as seen on the 1941 map of Wake, gives the impression of a well-thought-out and meticulously planned defense. And so it was, but it was more effective on paper than in reality. The overwhelming problem was insufficient manpower; there were not enough marines to operate all the weapons. They had fewer than half the number of men needed, so some of the guns were undermanned and some completely unmanned.

All the five-inch guns were manned, but only one had a full crew. Of the twelve antiaircraft guns, only six were manned. There were sufficient crews for only half the machine guns. Even those weapons that had enough men to fire them were limited by a shortage of tools and spare parts.

Only one of the three-inch batteries had its full fire-control equipment. Another battery lacked the all-important height finder and had to get information on the altitude of a target from another battery by telephone. Fortunately the five-inch guns had sufficient fire-control equipment, but there were almost no replacement parts for the delicate apparatus.

The air defense was worse. The three-inch guns, even had they had all the parts and men needed to operate them, were obsolete weapons. As Commander Cunningham put it, "they could neither reach high enough nor hit hard enough." Despite this weakness, they would take a deadly toll of enemy aircraft.

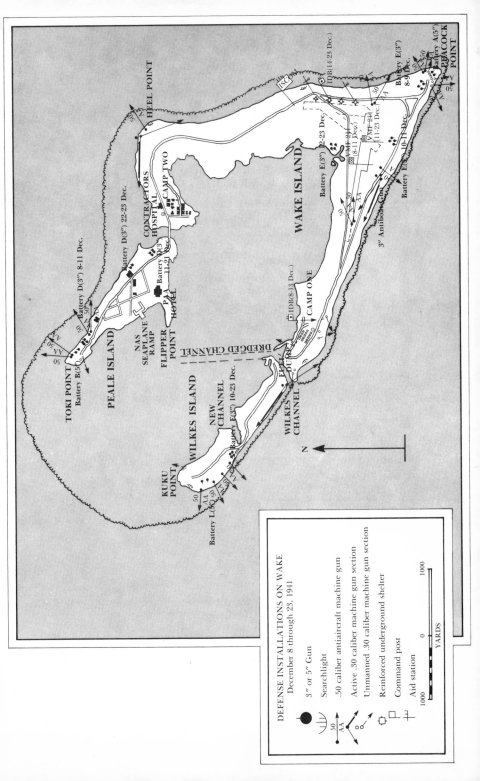

DEFENSE INSTALLATIONS ON WAKE
December 8 through 23, 1941

3" or 5" Gun

Searchlight

.50 caliber antiaircraft machine gun

Active .30 caliber machine gun section

Unmanned .30 caliber machine gun section

Reinforced underground shelter

Command post

Aid station

YARDS

1000   0   1000

Most important of all, there was no radar to warn of approaching planes. It had been promised but hadn't arrived. The only "early warning system" was an observation post on top of the fifty-foot water tower. There were no sound detectors for the searchlights, and with the continual roaring of the surf there was no way to detect approaching planes until they were almost over the island.

Another weak point was communications. The field telephone equipment was old, and the wires, frayed in spots, were all above ground where they could easily be damaged by bombs. There was neither enough time nor the right kind of equipment to bury the miles of wires. Also, the lines were in the open, close to the roads, and thus even more exposed. There was a primitive walkie-talkie network between command posts of the three islands, but it was not reliable. In spite of all the other problems Wake Island had, this may have been the most severe. Indeed, it is possible that Wake might not have fallen when it did had communications not failed during the Japanese invasion.

Work on the airfield continued at a feverish pace. Wake needed fighter planes to defend itself and patrol planes to report on what was over the horizon. Planners at Pearl Harbor were busy trying to provide both.

On December 3, a squadron of twelve navy PBY Catalina flying boats glided in to land on the lagoon at Wake. They had come to scout the ocean far around the atoll in advance of a small task force including the carrier *Enterprise* with its squadron of fighter planes for Wake. The PBYs stayed three days, and each morning six of them raced across the lagoon to fan out in search patterns. It was definite now—fighter planes were on their way!

The squadron selected to go to Wake Island was Marine Fighter Squadron 211, known in the Marine

Corps as VMF-211, under the command of Major Paul A. Putnam.* At thirty-eight, Putnam had a distinguished service record which included duty in the 1931 fighting in Nicaragua, where he had served with Devereux. Putnam was decorated by the Nicaraguan government and received a letter of commendation from the American secretary of the navy praising his tact and judgment. Quiet and soft-spoken, he was an energetic and determined squadron leader.

On the afternoon of November 27, Putnam and his men received secret verbal orders alerting them to be prepared to leave Pearl Harbor aboard a carrier. Their planes were F4F-3s (Grumman Wildcats), a type already becoming obsolete, but new to a squadron which only a few months before had been flying biplanes. Most of the pilots had no more than thirty hours flying time in their Wildcats. Quickly the bright peacetime colors of yellow, gray, and green, with white diagonal stripes across the wings, were covered with dull blue and gray camouflage paint.

On November 28, the planes took off from the marine air base (Ewa Mooring Mast) and flew to Ford Island in the middle of Pearl Harbor, and from there to the deck of the *Enterprise*. The mission had such a high priority that when one of the planes refused to start, its pilot was flown to the *Enterprise* and given one of the carrier's own Wildcats, circumventing miles of red tape. The transfer of the squadron was so fast that the pilots had nothing with them but toilet articles and one change of clothes when the *Enterprise* sailed that day.

War fever was running high at Pearl Harbor by then. The *Enterprise,* and every ship of the fleet, had been stripped down for battle in April 1941. The peacetime linoleum was removed from the deck, paint scraped off bulkheads, all flammable furniture and equipment taken

* V stands for aircraft (heavier-than-air), M for marine, and F for fighter.

off. Portholes were welded shut, and the entire ship painted dark gray. The task force for Wake, including three cruisers and nine destroyers, was commanded by Vice Admiral William "Bull" Halsey, and he expected war to explode at any moment.

On the first day at sea he told his crew, "At any time, day or night, we must be ready for instant action." Before leaving Pearl, he had been briefed by Admiral Kimmel, who stressed the need for absolute secrecy about the delivery of planes to Wake. The Japanese must not learn of it, Kimmel warned.

Halsey wanted to know what he should do if he met any Japanese ships.

"How far do you want me to go?" he asked Kimmel.

"Goddammit!" Kimmel yelled. "Use your common sense."

Halsey thought it was "the best order" he had ever been given, and he promised Kimmel that if he saw so much as a sampan he would sink it immediately.

As soon as the ships cleared Pearl Harbor, Halsey put the carrier under war alert. Live warheads were put on torpedoes, planes were fully loaded with bombs and ammunition, and pilots were ordered in no uncertain terms to shoot down any plane and sink any ship they saw. This was no training exercise.

When Halsey's operations officer saw the order to sink on sight anything afloat, he went to the admiral.

"Admiral, did you authorize this thing?" he asked.

"Yes."

"Goddammit, sir, you can't start a private war of your own. Who's going to take the responsibility?"

"I'll take it," Halsey replied. "If anything gets in my way, we'll shoot first and argue afterwards."

On the second day out Putnam was informed of his squadron's destination, and Halsey told him and the ship's personnel that "nothing should be overlooked nor any trouble spared" to make sure he got to Wake with his planes "in as near perfect condition as possible."

Mechanics worked day and night checking out the planes. "I feel a bit like the fatted calf," Putnam wrote to his superior, "being groomed for whatever it is that happens to fatted calves, but it surely is nice while it lasts." Although he was getting plenty of service and cooperation, Putnam still didn't know what he was supposed to do on Wake.

"My orders," he wrote, "are not so direct. In fact I have no orders."

After dinner one night, Putnam talked to Admiral Halsey.

"I know I'm on my way to Wake," he said, "but what in the hell am I supposed to do when I get there?"

"Putnam, your instructions are to do what seems appropriate when you get to Wake," the admiral said. "You're there under my direct and personal orders and will not report for duty to the island commander."

Putnam was then told that his squadron might be recalled from Wake as "suddenly and secretly" as it was being sent there. He was given a code word and informed that if he received it he should have his entire squadron airborne one hour after daybreak the following morning. A plane from the carrier would meet them and guide them back to the ship. Putnam was ordered not to mention the possibility of being recalled to anyone on Wake until "if and when necessary." It was all very mysterious.*

Halsey shook Putnam's hand.

"Have a pleasant cruise," he said.

On the morning of December 4, the task force reached a point some two hundred miles northeast of Wake. A PBY appeared on the horizon, one of those now based at Wake. The carrier turned into the wind,

---

* Putnam revealed these instructions in a letter to Cunningham in June, 1948.

and the twelve little snub-nosed fighters took off and followed the seaplane back to the atoll.

In less than two hours they zoomed over the island in V-formations of three planes each and came in for landings, one at a time, on the white coral runway. The whole island turned out to welcome them. Everyone, civilian and military alike—almost 1,700 men—lined the runway and parking apron and cheered as each plane made a perfect landing. "It was all a very impressive spectacle," wrote Major Bayler.

The presence of the planes was reassuring. The island now had eyes to see with and something more to fight back with. Though they did look "pretty sleek and fat," as Putnam described them, and were the first-line fighters of the Marine Corps in 1941, these early model F4F-3s left something to be desired. They were rugged planes, able to withstand a lot of punishment and keep flying, but they had no outstanding performance characteristics.*

The planes had no armor plate to protect the pilot and no self-sealing fuel tanks, even though the fighting in Europe had shown how vital these two improvements were. The fuel tanks were particularly critical since the main tank was located underneath the cockpit and the emergency tank was just behind the pilot's seat. Another outdated feature of the F4F-3 was the landing gear, which had to be cranked up and down by hand at a time when most other combat aircraft had power retraction systems. It was not unusual to see a Wildcat weaving from side to side shortly after takeoff as the pilot turned a crank thirty times with his right hand to raise the wheels. The cranking motion was transmitted through his body to his left hand, which held the control stick. When lowering the landing gear, the pilot had to grip

---

* They remained the first-line fighters only through the first five months of 1942, when a later model (F4F-4) replaced them.

the crank tightly lest it start spinning and break his wrist.

To add to these problems, the pilots were new to this type of plane and had no practice in tactical flying or in gunnery. They knew little about their engines and other technical matters. Nor was the ground crew in any better shape. None of the aviation section under Lieutenant Conderman was an experienced mechanic. No one was as yet familiar with the instruction manuals for the planes, and someone had forgotten to ship them along with the ground crew.

But the excited men on the ground at Wake on December 4 knew nothing of these problems, and it was just as well they didn't. They saw the snouts of the four .50 caliber machine guns in the wings of each plane and agreed with Commander Cunningham that "it was a cheering sight."

The lead plane taxied to the end of the runway, and Major Putnam stepped out, pushed his goggles up onto his leather flying helmet, and grinned as he shook hands with the welcoming committee. He watched the rest of his squadron land, then quickly went to work to learn about the situation.

Most of what he learned he didn't like, and most of what he didn't like he could see for himself with a glance around the unfinished airfield. He hadn't expected such primitive facilities and was not one to put up with them any longer than he could help it. The first thing he noticed was the landing strip itself. It was long enough, much longer than a Wildcat needed, but not wide enough to allow more than one plane at a time to take off. This would severely delay the scrambling of fighters in the event of air attack; the pilots wouldn't be able to get enough of them off the ground in time.

There were still no revetments or protective shelters of any kind. The planes had to stand out in the open. It was not even possible to disperse them widely around the field. The parking or hardstand mat areas were so rough that the planes could easily be damaged on them, even if they were pushed slowly by hand.

Nor were there any spare parts. Damage of a single part could completely disable a plane. They would soon have spare parts, but in a most unfortunate way—taking them from the wreckage of aircraft disabled on the first day of war. Fueling the planes involved the same tedious hand pump system used for the B-17s.

There was an adequate supply of hundred-pound bombs on Wake, but they were the wrong type for the F4F-3s. They wouldn't fit the bomb racks under the wings of the fighters. That problem was solved by improvisation, which Major Devereux said was "the basic industry of Wake Island." The ordnance officer of the squadron, Captain Herbert C. Freuler, took the supporting bands from the water-filled practice bombs and put them on the live hundred-pounders and thus was able to hang two bombs under the wing of each plane. No one knew for sure if it would work. There was always the chance that a bomb would not release, leaving the pilot with the unenviable job of landing with a live bomb.

Also lacking was the proper equipment to refill the oxygen bottles necessary for high altitude flight. Again Captain Freuler and his ground crew improvised a way to transfer oxygen from the storage tanks. It was a dangerous procedure, and one end of the airfield had to be cleared whenever the transfers took place. The danger of explosion was great, but there was no other way to get the job done.

The day after the squadron landed, Putnam instituted daily patrols at dawn and dusk, with four planes in each flight. They involved circling the island at a distance of fifty miles and were as necessary for training as for observation. Training in navigation and instrument flying was particularly crucial because the island was a small speck in the ocean, difficult to find, particularly through intermittent cloud banks. The pilots had to learn to locate the island on their own because there was no electronic homing or navigational equipment that could be used by the fighters.

On the ground, Putnam pushed for immediate construction of revetments and more and better hardstand areas, and he worked hard to make sure every plane and every man was ready for war.

On December 6, the twelve PBYs left Wake bound for Midway. Major Bayler, whose orders called for him to go to Midway as soon as he had completed his work on Wake, went to see the squadron commander to ask for a ride. His request was turned down. Each plane was already heavily loaded, the commander explained; there was no room for a passenger.

Bayler watched the planes take off and disappear over the horizon. Then he walked slowly to the officers' club and settled down with a bottle of cold beer to write a letter to his wife. She and their ten-year-old daughter were staying at a hotel in Honolulu where he would rejoin them after he set up the radio installation on Midway. He told her about his experiences on Wake and mentioned that he was now temporarily marooned there, waiting for a plane to take him on. There are, he wrote, "worse places than Wake Island to pass an enforced vacation. It's a beautiful spot; interesting, and so peaceful."

Others felt the same way that last weekend before the war. "Morale was high," Major Devereux wrote. "It was the only good weekend since I had landed on the island." Despite all that they lacked, the marines had accomplished much in a short period of time. They were confident that now, with guns in place and planes patrolling beyond the island, they could accomplish their mission and defend the island against short hit-and-run attacks from sea or air. They had plenty of food—a six-months' supply—ample water and medical supplies, and enough ammunition for limited operations. If they were attacked heavily, the great Pacific Fleet led by its eight massive battleships would come steaming out of Pearl Harbor to relieve them.

Commander Cunningham wrote that "the week drew to a close on almost a relaxed note." On Saturday morning, December 6, Devereux felt he could finally take the time to hold a general quarters drill for his defense battalion. The bugler blew Call to Arms, every gun which had an assigned crew was manned, communications were tested, and simulated targets tracked. It was the first such drill they had had, and while it did not include gunnery exercises—the first actual firing would be in combat—it was as close to war conditions as they could get.

Each man fell to with snap and precision, and Devereux was so pleased with their performance that he gave them the rest of the afternoon and all Sunday off—only their second Sunday holiday in more than two months. Word of the holiday spread quickly, and everybody else—contractors, pilots, air crew, and sailors at the naval air station—decided to take off too.

It was a happy weekend. The swimming pool was crowded, men fished off the reef, small boats went back and forth across the lagoon ferrying people from one island to another. They loafed or wrote letters or played cards. The outdoor movie was filled to capacity that night. Commander Cunningham played tennis with a young ensign who undiplomatically beat him. Shortwave radios pulled in stations from Hawaii and San Francisco, and homesick men heard "Take the A Train," "Elmer's Tune," "I Don't Want to Set the World on Fire," and other hits of the day.

The Pan American Clipper *Philippine* arrived on Sunday afternoon with mail for the garrison. The passengers stepped ashore to spend the night; they would leave for Guam in the morning. One passenger was to remain. Mr. H. P. Hevenor had been sent by the Bureau of the Budget to check on construction expenses and make sure the taxpayers were getting their money's worth.

Devereux and some of the other officers chatted with the passengers and listened to the latest rumors about the possibility of war. They were the same predictions that people had been making for years; it was no longer very frightening.

Time magazine wrote that the odds on war with Japan were now nine in ten. On December 6, Walter Lippmann wrote, "The country is now really on the verge of an actual all-out war." And in the morning papers of December 7, columnist Mark Sullivan said, "At the moment this is written we are extremely close to war with Japan."

"There was no use fretting," Major Devereux wrote, "because if you weren't stationed on this island, you'd be stationed on some other one. I think that was the way most of us felt on Wake the last night of peace."

4

"This Is No Drill!"

The sky was overcast on the morning of December 8,*
but even at 6:00 A.M. the air was warm with the pro-
mise of a hot, muggy day. In Camp 1, a solitary young
marine walked from his tent to a position close to the
flagpole and raised his bugle to his lips. Field Music
Alvin J. Waronker had never planned to be a bugler and
really didn't have too much talent for it. He volunteered
for Music School because the alternative was duty in
Alaska and he hated cold weather.

The brisk notes of reveille rang out over the marine
camp. Waronker tried hard, but some of the notes always sounded sour and off-key. He was kidded a lot
about it in a good-natured way—his bugle calls had become a favorite joke among the marines on Wake. The
men got up, well rested for the first time in months, and
made their way to the latrines and the mess hall.

Across the lagoon in the Pan American hotel, waiters
were serving breakfast to the Clipper passengers. They
ate silently, most of them unused to getting up so early.

---

* Wake is west of the international date line and is twenty-two hours ahead
of Hawaii. Thus, Sunday, December 7 at Pearl Harbor was Monday, December 8 on Wake. In the story of the siege, the dates used are those on
Wake Island.

They faced another long day flying over the vast, empty ocean. While they finished breakfast, their luggage was being carted out to the waiting plane. The pilot, Captain John Hamilton, checked the weather forecast while the ground crew readied the plane for its long flight. They were headed for Guam today, in the heart of Japanese territory.

In Camp 2, Dan Teters's construction workers were enjoying their usual hearty breakfast of bacon and eggs. Commander Cunningham, whose office was on Peale Island, ate with them and watched one burly man consume a dozen eggs.

In the marine mess hall, Major Bayler lingered over his breakfast wondering what he would do today. His job was finished, and all he could do was wait for a navy plane that could take him to Midway. Other marines finished their breakfast and went to their tents to square them away before reporting for work details.

The passengers left the hotel, walked along the white crushed coral path down to the dock, and took their seats in the plane. The steward checked to make sure seat belts were fastened. Captain Hamilton listened carefully to the sound of each engine as it started, checked his dials and gauges, and taxied out into the lagoon. The water was calm this morning, smooth and deep green in color, and the Clipper's hull knifed cleanly through it with hardly a bounce. They roared over Camp 1 and turned on a westerly course.

At 6:50 A.M. Major Devereux was in his tent shaving and mentally reviewing the order of work priorities for the day. Near the airstrip, in the small radio van used by the six-man army detachment, the radio operator was warming up his equipment. He twirled the receiver dial to the frequency used by the nearest United States Army air base, Hickam Field in Hawaii. He jerked up straight in his chair as a frantic message came through. It was in plain English, uncoded, and violated all the procedures for military transmission. He wrote it down and shouted for Captain Wilson, the head of the army team.

Wilson raced for Devereux's tent and burst inside without knocking. Wordless, he handed Devereux a piece of paper.

"Hickam Field has been attacked by Jap dive bombers!

"This is the real thing."

Devereux read it, then calmly rinsed the shaving cream off his face. He telephoned Commander Cunningham, but he was not yet in his office; then he called the navy radio station. He had to confirm the message from Hickam. There had been too many false alerts in the past months.

"Have you received a priority message from Pearl Harbor?" he asked the navy radioman.

"Yes sir. It's being decoded now."

That was all the confirmation Devereux needed. He left the tent and headed toward his office.

"Send me the Music on the double!" he yelled as he passed the guard tent.

When he entered the office, First Sergeant Paul Agar, on duty at his desk, started to say good morning.

"It's started," Devereux interrupted. "The Japs have attacked Pearl Harbor."

Sergeant Agar stared at him for a moment. "Well, I'll be god-damned," he said.

Field Music Waronker rushed into the office.

"Sound Call to Arms," Devereux told him.

Waronker ran outside and sounded the call that the marines had heard just two days before—the call to battle stations. The men thought it was another drill, and they laughed and joked as they went to their tents for rifles and helmets. Some even took time to wolf down the last of their breakfast. Devereux stood outside his office and watched with mounting anger.

"This is no drill!" he yelled to the nearest marines. "Pass the word!"

Some stared at him in disbelief, but not for long. In seconds everyone was moving on the double, running for the trucks that had assembled to take them to the gun stations. There was no more laughter. Up and down the rows of tents the word spread—"This is no drill!"

Devereux sent word for all officers of the defense battalion to report to him immediately, and within a half-hour they were crowded into his tiny office. In terse terms he told them what had happened—at least, what little he knew about it. Then he told them what they already suspected—they could expect to be attacked at any minute. If the Japanese could mount a bombing raid as far east as Hawaii, they would have no trouble doing the same thing to Wake. He ordered his officers to their battle stations.

The meeting lasted only a few minutes. The talk was straightforward, without emotion. There was nothing dramatic about it. They were professionals; they were marines, and this was the day they had spent years training for. Calmly, efficiently, they all went to work. Less than forty-five minutes after Devereux first received word of the Pearl Harbor attack, every post reported in that it was manned and ready.

At the airfield, Major Putnam heard the news just as the regular morning patrol was about to take off. He immediately ordered two more planes to join the patrol and set up a flight schedule that would keep four planes in the air at all times. Another four would be kept ready, with the remaining four undergoing maintenance checks. Putnam issued a string of orders, then climbed into the cockpit of his Wildcat and led Wake Island's first wartime patrol.

The airfield was frantic with activity. Men swarmed over the four relief planes loading hundred-pound bombs, fitting long belts of machine gun cartridges into the wings, and topping off the fuel tanks. The most pressing problem was to protect the eight planes on the ground. Work was under way on revetments, one for each plane, but they wouldn't be ready until 1:00 that afternoon. The buildings and tents containing stores and equipment were not camouflaged and could not be for another twenty-four hours. The smooth surfacing of parking aprons and access roads around the field, needed to properly disperse the planes, was in progress but wouldn't be ready until the next day. There were no foxholes or bomb shelters around the field, but men were busy at work on them. They would be finished by 1:00.

All that could be done with the planes was to disperse them as much as possible, to separate them so that several couldn't be destroyed by the same bomb. The ground crew pushed and shoved the 5,200-pound fighters to various points on the restricted parking area, but there were no more than fifty yards between them.

Shortly after the four Wildcats took off, a large plane suddenly appeared out of the west. The antiaircraft guns were already tracking it when word came through not to open fire. It was the Pan American Clipper returning. Shortly after he learned of the Pearl Harbor attack, Commander Cunningham had ordered the plane back to Wake, an action that saved the passengers and crew from being captured on Guam or possibly being shot down en route. Captain Hamilton circled gracefully and made a smooth landing in the lagoon. The passengers quickly disembarked and went to the hotel while Pan American officials awaited word on what to do about their flight schedule.

At 8:00 there occurred a ceremony that marines performed every morning all over the world—Morning Colors, the raising of the flag. Field Music Waronker had more trouble with that call—To the Colors—than any other. His discordant playing was particularly evident when he tried to blow the long, slow notes. But this morning was different. It was an experience that, as

Major Devereux wrote, "is hard to put into words. . . . we heard something none of us will ever be able to explain. I doubt even Waronker could. He just stood there and sounded off as the flag went up, and every note was proud and clear. It made a man's throat tighten to hear it. This time there were no wisecracks when the last note ended. It was the only time it ever happened."

The marines had stopped their work and come to attention facing the flagpole. Two privates pulled sharply on the halyards, and the flag was run smartly up the pole, unfurling and whipping in the breeze. They knelt and tied the halyards to the base of the pole. For a moment, as the last note of the bugle died away, there was a perfect stillness around Camp 1. No one moved, no one spoke; every eye was on the flag. Major Bayler remembered it as the "one truly emotional moment in those early hours of December 8." The flag remained until the Japanese lowered it sixteen days later.

Officers and men swarmed in and out of Devereux's office. There were scores of questions and details to be attended to. Additional ammunition was allotted to each position, and men and trucks assigned to pick it up and deliver it. Watches were set up at each gun battery. At least one gun in each battery had to be fully ready to fire on a moment's notice. The other gun crews got busy digging foxholes, stowing ammunition in bunkers, and filling the rapidly dwindling supply of sandbags.

The few spare rifles and pistols were distributed to the unarmed soldiers and sailors, but there weren't nearly enough guns to go around. And there were no helmets for any of them. Communications were checked and alternate lines laid. Provisions were made for getting food and water to the positions scattered all over the atoll. Command posts were set up away from the main areas so they would be less vulnerable in a bombing raid.

Lieutenant Gustav M. Kahn, the only navy doctor on the island, was ordered to take over the large civilian hospital at Camp 2, a bigger and better equipped facility than the marine aid station.

Amidst the officers and noncoms who streamed in and out of Devereux's office was a civilian. He stood rigidly at attention in front of Devereux's desk and in crisp parade-ground tones said, "Sir, Adams, former seaman United States Navy, reporting for duty. Sir, can you use me?"

Devereux could and did. And there were others who volunteered that morning from Dan Teters's crew, mostly men who had served in the armed forces. Commander Cunningham met with Commander Greey and Teters to discuss what to do about the civilian workers. Teters agreed that those who wanted to volunteer for work crews with the marines would be allowed to do so. The rest, scattered widely over Wake and Peale, were left to continue with their construction work. The fact that they were dispersed so widely would have to serve as their only protection for the moment.

At 9:30, the four planes of the morning patrol returned. The planes were quickly refueled and pushed to spots on the parking apron vacated by the four relief planes that sped down the runway one behind the other. They climbed to 12,000 feet and headed south, the most likely direction for an enemy raid. Rain squalls and intermittent cloud cover spotted the ocean beneath them. The pilots were on constant watch, eyes straining for any sign of Japanese planes.

About midway through their patrol, a flight of thirty-six Japanese bombers passed about 3,000 feet below them, hidden by a cloud bank. The planes were Air Attack Force No. 1 of the Twenty-Fourth Air Flotilla based at Roi-Namur, seven hundred miles to the south. They were on a direct course for Wake, to begin the first phase of the systematic destruction of the island's defenses—the softening-up process preparatory to invasion.

Shortly after the Wildcats had taken off, Major Devereux received another civilian visitor, Captain Hamilton, the pilot of the Pan American Clipper. As a result of a conversation with Commander Cunningham, Hamilton, a lieutenant in the Naval Reserve, had volunteered to fly a long-range reconnaissance flight south of Wake, covering a greater distance than the fighters could. Everyone agreed that it was a good idea, so Pan Am employees set to work unloading the plane's cargo to give it greater speed and range. Hamilton said he would be ready to leave by 1:00 that afternoon.

Wake was alive and bustling with activity. The slight figure of Major Devereux seemed to be everywhere at once as he personally checked on all the last-minute preparations for war. Major Putnam was all over the airfield urging his men on. Gasoline was transferred into drums for storage around the landing strip, ammunition was linked together in the long chains needed to feed the fighters' .50 caliber machine guns, armorers and mechanics worked feverishly on the eight planes left on the ground. On Peale Island, Commander Cunningham, back from a quick tour of the atoll's state of readiness, conferred with Dan Teters about other defensive preparations the civilians could work on.

And all over the atoll men cast quick glances at the southern sky and listened, straining for the sound of aircraft engines. They heard nothing but the surf. In the tiny observation platform atop the water tower, the two men on duty cursed as they saw the drifting rain squall a half-mile to the south. They had no shelter from the rain up there.

At 10,000 feet, the Japanese flight leader saw the same squall line and decided to take advantage of it. He signaled to the three twelve-plane V-formations, and they started to descend.

In his office, Devereux sat down at his desk and made a phone check of all positions. Every battery was as ready as it could possibly be. The observation post reported no planes in sight. On Peale Island, Commander Cunningham and Dan Teters were still checking off the list of priorities. The Pan American passengers were sitting down to lunch in the hotel. On the parking apron at the airfield, Majors Putnam and Bayler, Lieutenant Conderman, four other pilots, and two clerks were lounging outside the squadron tent waiting for lunch to be served.

It was 11:58 A.M.

The Japanese planes came out of the rain squall almost directly over the southern end of the atoll. They bore in midway between Camp 1 and Peacock Point at an altitude of 2,000 feet. The bomb bay doors were open and the first bombs already dropping before anyone on the ground saw them. The attack was a complete surprise.

Out on the end of Wake in Battery E, First Lieutenant Wally Lewis happened to look up at the instant the planes crossed the beach. He reached for the telephone to call Major Devereux. A civilian standing nearby yelled, "Look, their wheels are falling off." Lewis knew better, and he shouted into the phone, "They're dropping bombs!"

At the airfield, someone in the group outside the squadron tent pointed to the planes and said, "Those must be our B-17s."

"B-17s, hell!" a young pilot answered. "Those aren't our planes! They're Japs."

All along the southern beach of Wake, the .50 caliber machine guns opened fire on the planes within seconds, and both of Lieutenant Lewis's three-inch antiaircraft guns went into action, but even that was too late.

Major Bayler and the group outside the squadron tent began to run south toward a patch of woods two hundred feet away. It was the only cover anywhere around the airfield. Bayler looked up and saw the planes directly overhead. He dove headfirst into the thick scrub and threw himself flat on the ground under a small tree.

The planes flew straight for the airfield, strafing everything in sight with their .20-millimeter guns, spraying incendiary bullets into every target. A closely spaced pattern of hundred-pound fragmentation bombs systematically tore the area to pieces. The air quickly filled with thick choking clouds of dust and burning gasoline. The heat grew intense as the 25,000-gallon high-octane aviation gas tank roared open in an explosion of liquid fire. All around the field, the 50-gallon drums burst into flame.

The screams of wounded men filled the air. Some were frantically trying to drag themselves out of the open area. Others sat up with dazed looks on their faces, trying to stop the blood spurting from their bodies.

There was a momentary lull, then the second V-formation fell upon them. Another wave of incendiary bullets and bombs showered the field. Four American pilots ran to their planes to try to take off. They raced across the field while bullets kicked up coral and sand at their feet. Lieutenant Frank Holden lurched, then fell, his body ripped to pieces by shrapnel. Lieutenant Harry Webb was next; he was hit in the stomach and both feet. There were two left—Lieutenants Graves and Conderman—running, zigzagging, heads bent. Miraculously Graves reached his plane and pulled himself up into the cockpit. A moment later a bomb scored a hit and tore the plane apart. Within seconds, the Wildcat's two bombs exploded. Then a thousand machine gun bullets began to fire as the flames reached the wings of what was left of the plane.

Lieutenant Conderman had almost made it to his plane when he was hit. Two marines braved the explosions and ran toward him to help.

"Let me go," Conderman said, and he pointed to the other wounded who littered the field. "Take care of them," he said, knowing he was dying.

Master Technical Sergeant Andrew Paszkiewicz, a twenty-year veteran, was hit in the leg and crawled through the hail of falling bombs to a nearby pile of debris. He fumbled through the wreckage and pulled out a piece of wood. Painfully he hauled himself up on his feet and, using the stick as a crutch, hobbled back into the path of the bombs, trying to help those more seriously wounded.

The planes swung across the lagoon to bomb Camp 2 and the Pan American station on Peale Island. The hotel and the seaplane facilities were hit, and bullets laced the wings and the fuselage of the Clipper. At Camp 2, a large number of construction workers had gathered for lunch; they were easy targets. Then one formation broke away from the others and came back over Camp 1 and the airfield again.

In twelve minutes it was over. The Japanese left without the loss of a single plane. An observer with the Japanese wrote that "the pilots in every one of the planes were grinning widely. Everyone waggled his wings to signify 'BANZAI.' "

Smoke rose in thick, oily columns from several scattered points on the atoll, but it was heaviest at the airfield. For a few minutes it hid the damage, but as it began to clear, the shambles left by the raid was revealed. Bright gasoline fires seemed to be everywhere, and so were dead and wounded men. Seven of the eight fighter planes caught on the ground were flaming torches from nose to tail, and the eighth was damaged. Major Putnam had been slightly injured and dazed by concussion, but he stayed to help the wounded. Blood spotted his uniform, and his face grew white with rage as the enormity of the destruction became apparent.

Of the fifty-five men in VMF-211, only twenty-one survived the raid unscathed. In those twelve minutes, sixty percent of the squadron had been killed or wounded; the final toll was twenty-three dead and eleven wounded. All the tents and buildings around the airfield had been destroyed, along with all the maintenance equipment for the planes and Major Bayler's air-to-ground radio equipment.

Later, after the wounded had been evacuated to the civilian hospital at Camp 2, Majors Putnam and Bayler talked about how systematic the bombing had been. They paced off the distances between the bomb craters and found them to be almost identical—fifty feet between each crater. They also noticed that the landing strip itself was virtually intact, although everything around it was in ruins. It was obviously carefully planned that way; the Japanese were saving the airstrip for their own use.

There was another surprise for marine aviation on Wake that morning when the four planes of the patrol returned, having made no contact with the enemy bombers. The pilots zoomed over the island and stared in shock at the devastation they saw. The first three planes landed without mishap, but the fourth struck its propeller on some debris that had been blown onto the airstrip. The prop was bent and the engine jarred in its mounts. Now all that remained of the marines' air defense were three flyable planes and two in need of repairs.

Camp 1 had also been hit heavily. Scores of tents were destroyed—including the officers' club, officers' mess, and enlisted men's mess—but there were no casualties among the men of the defense battalion, most of whom were scattered about the atoll at various gun positions.

None of the gun batteries had been attacked; their turn would come later.

The damage on Peale Island was as extensive as that at the airfield. Some Pan American fuel tanks had been blown up, along with the radio station, machine shop, and the hotel. Hardly a structure remained standing in the Pan Am compound. A bomb had killed ten Pan Am employees, all Chamorros from Guam, and wounded some others. Somehow the passengers all survived, and so did the Clipper. The big silver flying boat sustained no major damage though there were bullet holes all through it, and mechanics quickly agreed that it could fly.

The only other military casualties were two sailors who were killed along with a civilian volunteer close to the Wilkes channel. At Camp 2, several buildings were hit and as many as fifty civilian construction workers killed or wounded. It was impossible to determine the exact number because immediately after the raid a number of the civilians fled for remote areas of undergrowth, taking food and supplies, and were not seen again until the surrender.

The somber task of collecting the dead took place after the wounded had been attended to. There was no time to bury them—there was too much work to do—and so they were placed in the large cold storage boxes at Camp 2.

On Peale Island, when the manager of the Pan American base, John B. Cooke, surveyed the damage to his equipment and facilities, he decided to evacuate all twenty-six Pan Am personnel. The outbreak of war meant that regular passenger flights would be canceled "for the duration," and so there was no reason for them to stay on Wake and risk death. He instructed the pilot, Captain Hamilton, to be ready to leave by 1:00 and set out to round up passengers and employees. The Clipper was stripped of nonessential items, including the mail. The remaining Chamorros, even though they worked for Pan American, were not allowed on the plane, and two who tried to stow away were kicked off. "It seemed," said Commander Cunningham, "an unfortunate time to draw the color line."

Shortly after 1:00 the heavily loaded plane eased away from the damaged dock and wallowed toward the channel. The extra weight made it more difficult to control in the water, and Captain Hamilton looked down the length of the channel and hoped it was long enough. He pushed the throttles, and the giant plane began slowly moving forward. The plane moved a third of the way across the lagoon, then halfway; the beach on the other side of the lagoon was coming closer and closer. Hamilton pushed the throttles hard, holding them in place, fighting for another fraction of an inch of forward movement, but it didn't help. They were running out of channel, and the plane's hull could not break free of the water.

Sharply he pulled the throttles back, and the plane quickly lost speed. He tried again, starting at a point as close to the beach as he dared maneuver the thin hull. Once again the weight was too much for the plane's engines, and he chopped the throttles in time to avoid ramming the beach on the other side of the lagoon. On the third try the hull finally broke free of the water, and the plane roared perilously low over Wake on its way to Midway. Everyone on the atoll had been watching, and they cheered as it flew over Camp 1.

As it disappeared to the northeast, two men watched in horror as they saw their chance of escape disappearing. A Pan American mechanic, August Ramquist, busy since the raid helping to get the wounded Chamorros to the hospital at Camp 2, didn't get the word about the flight. Nor did Mr. Hevenor, the visitor from the Bureau of the Budget, who had wisely decided to leave on the Clipper. Somehow he missed seeing the departure notice. Both men became prisoners of the Japanese—"a rather drastic lesson in the wisdom of punctuality," Major Devereux drily noted.

At the airfield, Major Putnam was reorganizing what was left of VMF-211. Gradually the gasoline fires were burning themselves out, and the last of the ammunition and bombs in the wrecked planes had exploded. Debris was cleared off the landing strip and the squadron's three remaining Wildcats took off to search for enemy planes and to make sure they weren't caught on the ground.

The men worked to salvage usable parts from the wrecked planes and tried to put the two damaged fighters in flying condition. Foxholes and bomb shelters were dug all around the field, and construction of the uncompleted protective revetments for the planes continued. New assignments were made to replace the morning's casualties. Replacing Lieutenant Graves as engineering officer was Second Lieutenant John F. Kinney. Together with Technical Sergeant William J. Hamilton, an enlisted pilot, he found some tools and parts in Camp 2 that could be used, or improvised for use, on the planes. In the coming days the two men would perform miracles in keeping the planes flying.

To protect the airstrip from an airborne invasion, heavy dynamite charges were planted every 150 feet along the runway. Bulldozers were brought over from Camp 2 to tear gaps and furrows in the clear ground adjacent to the field to prevent Japanese planes from landing. Road graders and other heavy construction equipment were brought to the edge of the runway, ready to be parked across the strip at night to prevent surprise landings. Major Putnam scheduled three regular patrols during daylight hours, at dawn, noon, and dusk.

On all three islands, the construction and repair activities continued throughout the afternoon. Commander Cunningham and Major Devereux had scores of problems to be resolved and not enough marines and sailors to do the job. The majority of the construction workers were of no help, but fortunately about 185 of them, along with Dan Teters, immediately placed themselves at the disposal of the military. They and more than one hundred others who later joined them were of immense help over the next fifteen days and were partly responsible for the atoll holding out as long as it did. Teters not only kept the volunteers on the contractor's payroll, but he also released equipment and supplies wherever needed. Other workers continued on their assigned project—building the naval air station.*

Marines and civilian workmen swarmed over the individual gun emplacements digging more foxholes and bomb shelters, improving camouflage and sandbag protection. One of the navy lighters was filled with concrete blocks and dynamite and anchored in the center of the Wilkes channel to prevent small boats from entering the lagoon. Damaged telephone lines were repaired, permanent command posts built, and covered latrines dug near the gun batteries on all three islands. The six-month supply of food was moved from its warehouse and stored in camouflaged dumps throughout the atoll. Empty gasoline drums were cleaned, filled with fresh water, and stored at various points.

The civilians also took on one of Devereux's biggest problems—feeding the now permanently dispersed

* By the time of Wake's capture, more civilians worked and fought beside the military. Commander Cunningham noted in his book that the number of such civilians cited by name by the military survivors of Wake totals 312. That includes only those whose names could be recalled. However, the fact remains that the majority of the civilians did not participate in the fighting and also refused to do any construction work to aid in the defense. They hid in the scrub during the entire siege. It was largely because of this experience that the navy organized the famous Sea–Bees (construction battalions), which were trained both to build and to fight.

marines. Not enough of his men could be spared from their guns to do the job, so Dan Teters volunteered to assume the whole operation of preparing and distributing food. Not knowing how long it might take for additional supplies to reach Wake, Devereux decided to ration food to two meals a day.

A crew of twenty-five civilians set up a permanent camp at Peacock Point to help with the gun batteries. In the coming days they worked alongside the marines repairing bomb damage and undertook all the work involved in handling ammunition for the five-inch battery. Other civilians volunteered to stand watch along with the marines. Still others learned as much as they could about the weapons so they could pitch in if marines were hit. Sixteen civilians went to Peale Island, where Sergeant W. A. Bowsher, Jr., a veteran marine, trained them as a gun crew to serve on the previously unmanned three-inch antiaircraft battery.

Major Devereux checked and double-checked everything, shifting men and machine guns around, trying to stretch his small force along the full length of exposed beach. On Wake Island, a detachment of seventy-three men was formed under the command of Second Lieutenant A. R. Poindexter to defend the area around Camp 1. It was a makeshift force composed of those few marines who did not have an essential combat post, clerks, cooks, and the sailors who had run the small boats in the channel. A mobile reserve force was formed with twelve of Poindexter's most experienced marines and four machine guns mounted on a truck.

The preparations continued all night though they had to be carried out under blackout conditions. The surviving VMF-211 members and some civilian volunteers completed eight blastproof revetments which would protect the planes from everything but a direct hit. Men were still trying to repair the plane that had damaged its propeller in landing.

Exhausted marines slept fitfully in foxholes and shelters that night, taking short naps interspersed with their work to prepare for whatever might lie ahead of them tomorrow. "We had taken a beating," Major Devereux wrote, "and we knew that first raid was only a curtain raiser." Everyone knew the Japanese would return with more planes and more bombs. And without radar, there was little hope of detecting them early enough even to get to a foxhole! But the men on Wake Island also knew they would do the best they could with what they had. If the Japanese wanted Wake, they would have to pay dearly for it.

The men knew there would be more bombings every day until the defenses were shattered, and then an invasion. It was inevitable. "Perhaps we would be reinforced before then, as most of us expected," Major Devereux said, "but we could not depend on it. We could depend only on ourselves, on our ability to make up by improvisation for our lack of men and equipment."

A cold drizzle began to fall. At what was left of the naval air station, Commander Cunningham thought over the day's losses, took stock of their meager resources, and reread the message he had received that afternoon from Pearl Harbor.

"Execute unrestricted submarine and air warfare against Japan."*

The second day of war dawned bright and clear. General Quarters sounded at 5:00 A.M., and all over the atoll marines stumbled out of foxholes and shelters, red-eyed from lack of sleep. Breakfast and hot coffee were distributed to the men, and quickly the work resumed. Every man was busy at something, and mostly it involved digging in. Major Devereux said, "Getting un-

---

* There were two submarines in the vicinity of Wake—*Triton* and *Tambor*—but they played no role in the defense of the atoll.

derground was an intensely personal problem."

A Condition 1 alert was set, which meant that all phones, weapons, and fire-control equipment were manned and battle lookouts were posted. At the airfield, the Wildcats' engines were being warmed up, and the marines were grateful to see four of the stubby little fighters ready to take off. Kinney and Hamilton had repaired the plane that survived the bombing raid and were still working hard to get the fifth plane, the one with the bent propeller, ready to fly. The planes roared down the runway at 5:45 and began their search around the island.

By 7:00, Devereux relaxed the alert status to Condition 2, which kept crews at only half the guns. The rest were required to remain close by, but they could resume the defensive work—and there was plenty yet to be done. Shelters were unfinished at the airfield and the gun batteries. On Wilkes, a detail of civilians and marines filled 500 sandbags to be placed around the antiaircraft guns. At the airfield, Major Putnam decided that the squadron's maintenance problems were so severe—and likely to get worse—that they needed a sheltered hangar where they could work all night under blackout conditions. Using one of Dan Teters's bulldozers, he cut ramps into two of the revetments and put roofs of I-beams, wood, and lightproof tarpaulins over them. Now a plane could be serviced at any hour of the day or night and be hidden from the air.

The morning patrol landed at 7:30. After refueling, two pilots, Lieutenant David D. Kliewer and Sergeant Hamilton, were sent up to serve as the Combat Air Patrol (CAP), staying close to the island. Their purpose was to be ready to break up an enemy attack.

As the morning wore on, the men stayed near their foxholes and kept watch for the first sign of enemy planes. It was not difficult to predict the approximate time the planes might arrive; based on flying time from the enemy bases in the Marshall Islands, if the planes took off at dawn, they would be over Wake shortly after 11:00 A.M.

The men assigned to the antiaircraft guns were particularly anxious to see the bombers. Except for the marine pilots, they were the only ones on the island with a chance to fight back, and they were eager to do so. In the raid the day before, the Japanese planes had flown too low for effective three-inch fire, and there was considerable discussion among the gunners as to what they would do today. Would they come in low again or bomb from a higher altitude? Lieutenant Lewis, commanding Battery E at Peacock Point, said flatly that the planes would come in high because even though the previous day's antiaircraft fire had been ineffective, there had been a great deal of it. That, Lewis said, would make them fly higher today, where they'd feel safe. But, he added, they wouldn't be safer. He was right.

At approximately 11:30, south of the atoll, Lieutenant Kliewer and Sergeant Hamilton spotted a formation of twin-tailed two-engine bombers flying straight for Wake. The two Wildcats pivoted and went into screaming dives as they tore into the bombers. The Japanese returned a heavy fire, but the fighters wheeled around and came back with their .50 caliber machine guns blazing. It was the first time any of the squadron pilots had fired from an F4F-3, and they did a good job of it. Smoke started to pour from one of the bombers, and the Wildcats pounced on it again and sent it spinning and flaming into the sea. Suddenly explosions appeared all around them—it was the flak from Wake's three-inch guns—and the fighters quickly climbed out of range. It was 11:45 when the formation appeared over Peacock Point.

This time the defenders had a warning. High up in the observation tower, Marine Gunner H. C. Borth, promoted from gunnery sergeant just two days before, spotted the planes closing fast at 13,000 feet. He yelled his report into the phone, and in seconds quick bursts of three shots, the signal for an air raid, were heard all over the atoll.* Men raced for their foxholes and shelters while the antiaircraft gunners began tracking the planes.

The first line of bombs crashed down on Peacock Point all around the heavy five-inch guns, showering dirt and debris among the foxholes. Black puffs of ack-ack spotted the air around the formation. The planes came over the airfield, and a line of bombs fell along the northern side of the runway churning up sand and coral, but finding no vital targets this time. A few fifty-gallon gasoline drums burst into flame, but the two remaining aircraft on the field were safe.

Major Devereux stood outside his command post watching the planes swing over the airfield. Suddenly, out of the smoke and dust, a gasoline truck appeared, racing along the edge of the runway. Bombs exploded all around it, and the driver savagely twisted the wheel from side to side. The truck lurched and turned sharply as the driver tried to outguess the Japanese bombardiers. Many men stopped to watch, disregarding their own safety for the moment, drawn irresistibly to the dramatic race against death. The truck turned again, a sharp sliding turn, but it was a wrong guess. The next bomb fell directly on it, and the truck disintegrated in a shower of flame and torn metal. Three marines had been in the truck; their remains were not found for ten days.

The enemy planes turned away from the airfield and headed across the lagoon in the direction of Camp 2. A few marines cheered as they saw smoke trailing from one of the planes, but it held its place in the formation.

---

* Wake did not have an air raid siren. A makeshift one was built out of automobile horns and batteries, but it proved to be ineffective. Three shots, fired in rapid succession, became the standard air raid alarm.

In one building in the contractor's camp, a group of men, civilian and military, exchanged anxious looks as they heard the drone of planes coming closer. It was a T-shaped, one-story wooden structure with a large red cross painted on the roof. The sick and wounded lay helpless as the roar of the engines grew louder, and they stared at the thin ceiling knowing it offered no protection at all. On Wake Island, a group of marines stood at the edge of the lagoon and watched the bombs fall toward the buildings of Camp 2.

"Them poor bastards," one of them said quietly.

Corpsmen and doctors placed those patients who could be moved under beds, then took cover themselves. Suddenly the building shook and dissolved in swirling, choking dust and debris as a bomb gutted one end. Showers of steel fragments sliced through the air. Lieutenant Henry G. "Spider" Webb was delirious with fever and didn't know what was happening around him. Just before the bombs hit, he reached for a metal water pitcher next to his bed. He picked it up, and water spurted from holes as shrapnel cut through it. Lieutenant Kahn, the navy doctor, crawled out from under a bed unhurt and looked down at a pair of shoes inches away. They had been cut to shreds.

Lieutenant Kahn, the civilian contractor's doctor Lawton M. Shank, and the navy corpsmen began dragging the screaming injured men out of the building.* Flames leaped up around them, but they returned to pull out more men. When everyone had been removed, they went back in again to save what medical supplies they could.

Virtually every building in Camp 2 had been damaged—the civilian barracks, the naval air station person-

---

* Dr. Shank won high praise from the marines for his coolness under fire. After the war, he was recommended for a Navy Cross, to be awarded posthumously.

nel quarters, machine shops, storehouses, a large garage, and the communications buildings. Many of the contractor's men still had not learned the value of dispersing during a raid; fifty-five died that morning in Camp 2.

Commander Keene and Dan Teters had a close call. When the bombing started, they ran inside a solid storage vault and closed the steel door behind them. After the raid they tried to open the door, but it had been bent by the force of the explosions and wouldn't budge. With help from outside, they finally got it open.

Peale Island was the next target for the Japanese bombers, and again, closely patterned bombs caused widespread destruction. The unfinished naval air station was battered heavily, and the aerological building, hangar, and radio station were gutted, along with a warehouse containing $1,000,000 worth of supplies. But by that time, five of the bombers were leaving smoke trails. As they headed out over the ocean, one plane erupted in a ball of flame, then disintegrated in a fiery explosion. Wake had claimed its second enemy. The other four damaged aircraft were still smoking when the formation disappeared from view.*

In the aftermath of the raid, the familiar, tedious, and painful process of cleaning up began. The wounded must be treated, the dead collected and identified, and wreckage searched for salvageable items. The marines were luckier this time—only four were killed.

Amazingly the deaths at the hospital were few; three patients had been killed. While some patients suffered additional wounds, they owed their lives to the courage of the medical staff. The redoubtable Sergeant Paszkiewicz was slightly injured again, and he let out a string of profanity while the doctors worked on him out

---

* A Japanese report studied after the war indicated damage to fourteen planes during that raid.

in the open. There was no longer a hospital, and most of the surgical equipment had been destroyed.

Safer facilities had to be found. Commander Cunningham decided to use two of the ammunition magazines east of the airfield for new hospitals, and work began at once to remove the shells and powder stored there. The magazines were igloo-shaped and made of reinforced concrete and steel. Built partially underground, they were the safest places on the atoll.

There were four of these magazines, widely separated in a line, and the two at either end were chosen as hospital sites. Each one had room for twenty-one beds and its own generator sheltered in a pit alongside. Dr. Shank was to serve in one for the civilian wounded, and Dr. Kahn in the other for the military. Shifting the ammunition to scattered points over the island and moving beds, patients, and supplies was a long hard job which took the men until nightfall to complete.

At the same time, another group of civilians and marines emptied a third magazine for use as something almost as vital. The Pan American and naval air station radio facilities had been destroyed. The atoll's only link to the outside world was Captain Wilson's Army Air Corps radio. It had been sitting in a van in the woods east of the airfield, much too vulnerable a spot.

Wilson, his small army team, and their equipment were moved into the third igloo. A young ensign, Cunningham's communications officer, moved in with them, and before long the igloo became the nerve center for the entire atoll as well as Cunningham's command post. That afternoon after the radio facility had been installed, Major Bayler and several other officers whose families were in Honolulu gathered around the radio while the operator sent out a CQ call, an invitation for anyone to answer. The operator also had relatives in Hawaii and, like the others, was worried about their safety.

News from Pearl Harbor had been skimpy, and none of the men knew how much of the area around the naval base and the city of Honolulu had been destroyed. Bayler, Captain Herbert Freuler, and others waited anxiously for an answer, and finally an operator in Hilo, 250 miles from Pearl Harbor, replied. The little group huddled close to the radio as the Wake operator identified himself and told where he was calling from. He asked for news about casualties and damage to Pearl and Honolulu. There was a pause, and when the man in Hilo answered, his voice was terse and suspicious. Hawaii was rife with spy scares; a voice over the radio was not to be trusted.

"No dope," the man said, and promptly signed off. It was a tremendous disappointment to the men on Wake Island and the closest they would come to finding out about their families. Quietly they filed out of the igloo and went back to work.

One of the three-inch antiaircraft guns in Battery E at Peacock Point had been damaged in the raid, and Devereux ordered Marine Gunner Clarence B. McKinstry to take the eight-ton weapon to Wilkes Island and bring back an undamaged one from the unmanned battery there. While this was going on, Devereux analyzed the two days of bombing and discovered a sequence which the enemy raids seemed to be following. The first day they had aimed for the fighter defenses. The second day it was the naval air station and that three-inch battery at Peacock Point that had opened fire immediately during the first raid.

Devereux was becoming increasingly concerned about the battery and was convinced that the Japanese would make a special effort to destroy it in the next raid. Gunner McKinstry reported that during the bombing that morning, one plane had circled their position. He believed they were taking photographs so they would be able to hit it accurately the next day. With these factors in mind, Devereux agreed with McKinstry's recommendation to move all four of the battery's guns 600 yards northeast of its present location, even though this would mean the guns couldn't fire on enemy aircraft until they were actually over the island.

It was a logical decision, and it turned out to be a wise one, but it required long hours of hard work which the marines couldn't begin until nightfall in case a Japanese observation plane should appear during the day and note the new location. Also, it was too big a job for the marines to accomplish alone in such a short time, so Dan Teters was once again asked for help. And once again he responded. At dusk he assembled a crew of a hundred men with trucks, and they descended upon Battery E.

No lights could be used at all. The outrigger legs on which each gun rested were folded inward; then it was jacked up so that a two-wheeled bogie (a dolly) could be rolled under it. The gun was jacked down so that it rested on the bogie platform, and it was made secure. A huge truck towed the gun to its new position, where it was taken off the bogie and set on the ground. Sandbags were filled and set in place, the guns camouflaged, and all the ammunition hauled from the old site to the new and placed in piles of a hundred rounds each near each gun.

At the old site, dummy guns were built of wood and the sandbags and camouflage replaced so that from the air nothing would appear to have changed. The sky was already beginning to lighten by the time the job was finished, and it was only a few minutes before General Quarters sounded that the men dispersed to try to get some sleep before the next raid.

That same night, Commander Cunningham received another helpful message from Pearl Harbor.

"All hands should wear long pants instead of shorts, in order to avoid burns from bomb blasts."

By Wednesday, December 10, the world of war on Wake Island had already become a routine. Peacetime habits and duties seemed long forgotten as men began to accept as normal the daily bombing, sleeping and eating in foxholes, and the ever present sight of wreckage and destruction.

At 10:45 A.M., twenty-six bombers appeared. They were flying higher than the day before—at 18,000 feet—and coming from the east instead of the south. The Americans on the ground were ready, more so than before, because for the first time all the ack-ack batteries were manned—after a fashion. Earlier that morning, Devereux had sent Gunner McKinstry to Wilkes Island to man Battery F with a crew of sailors, civilians, and one other marine. The battery had no fire-control equipment, and the guns even lacked sights, so they were of limited value against aircraft. They were primarily for the defense of the beach, but at least they gave the impression of greater firepower.

Before the enemy planes reached the atoll, the Wildcats pounced on them. Captain Hank Elrod shot down two of the bombers before he and the other fighters had to peel off to avoid Wake's ack-ack fire. The first wave of bombers headed directly for the dummy guns set up where Battery E had been the day before. A string of bombs rained down, obliterating two of the wooden guns and barely missing the others, but near enough to have knocked the real guns out of action had they been there.

One formation swung out toward Peale Island and made two passes over Battery D, another set of four antiaircraft guns. Just as the planes came over, the battery's power plant failed; the mechanism that enabled the gunners to predict the path of a plane would not work. The gunners fired the weapons anyway, aiming by sight, and threw up enough shells to keep the enemy at a high altitude. The bombardiers' aim was thrown off, and most of the bombs fell harmlessly into the lagoon or beyond the reef. When the planes turned away, the gunners could see smoke coming from one of them.

It was Wilkes'Island, isolated and almost empty, that received the heaviest bombardment that day. One bomb fell on a construction company shed which housed 125 tons of dynamite. The resulting explosion was the most spectacular anyone had ever seen. The roar drowned out the pounding surf, and coral, sand, and debris were blown over all three islands. Every bit of vegetation on Wilkes was stripped bare, and then the denuded trees and shrubs spontaneously burst into flame. A second later, every piece of ammunition on the island exploded. Both of the five-inch guns and one of the antiaircraft guns were severely damaged. The thick gun barrels were dented, firing locks and other parts stripped off, and all the fire-control apparatus ruined. A searchlight truck a half-mile away was wrecked. Miraculously only one marine was killed and four wounded, although everyone on Wilkes was badly shaken up.

Aside from the damage on Wilkes, it was the least costly raid so far—two dead and six wounded. But the enemy had lost two planes, and a third was damaged. Morale among the men was high when word of the low casualties reached them, and they pitched into their work that afternoon with renewed vigor. Broken telephone lines were again repaired, the faulty power plant in the battery on Peale was replaced by one of Dan Teters's diesel generators, and Major Devereux moved his command post into a newly built bomb shelter near the beach.

On Wilkes, Gunner McKinstry moved his position closer to the shore and camouflaged it with burned brush, though he did not have sandbags to protect the crews. The damaged five-inch guns on Wilkes were repaired as best they could be. The marines hoped that the guns would still fire, but aiming them properly would be difficult.

At the airfield, the Combat Air Patrol was kept up all day, with the four Wildcats operating in relays of two. In the enclosed hangar, Kinney and Hamilton reported that they might soon have a fifth plane ready to fly. That night Battery E was moved again, this time to a spot on the lagoon side of Wake, and new dummy guns were set up in the battery's old position.

In spite of all that had happened, there was a spirit of optimism in the air that afternoon and evening of December 10. Commander Cunningham wrote: "We were shaken and hungry and so tired we could fall asleep on our feet, but the situation was definitely looking up. Four of their bombers had definitely been destroyed. We had dug in. We were learning about war and how to take care of ourselves—the hard way, but a way that was an effective teacher. . . . and we had discovered that a man's chances of surviving an air raid were pretty good if he observed normal precautions. We were growing accustomed to our new way of life; we felt better than we had at any time since our Sunday holiday."

As the sun set that evening, the sky over Wake was clear. A hundred or so miles to the south, however, the weather was quite different; a violent storm was in progress. The heavy seas and high winds lashed fiercely at a small convoy of ships. The task force, headed by Rear Admiral Kajioka, was carrying a special landing force of 450 men. Tomorrow they would invade Wake Island.

5

"Send Us More Japs"

Two thousand miles east of Wake Island in an office overlooking the wreckage of the once mighty Pacific Fleet, Admiral Kimmel and his staff were trying desperately to wring some semblance of order out of the chaos that surrounded them. There was no mistaking the magnitude of the catastrophe. The evidence was painfully obvious, from burnt skeletons of planes on the airfields to the oily waters of the harbor. Thick clouds of black smoke still stained the blue sky, and rescue workers continued to hear tapping noises from inside the hull of the capsized battleship *Arizona*.

On Monday, December 8, the day after the Pearl Harbor attack, the admiral's staff still wore the same dress white uniforms they had been wearing when the first bombs fell. They were haggard and unshaven, some were taking sedatives on surgeon's orders, and a few men's hair had turned white overnight. Admiral Kimmel, always impeccably tailored, sat in his wrinkled uniform, and his eyes were dazed. Vice Admiral Pye, Kimmel's assistant and an ardent defender of the battleship, was numb and bewildered. Neither man yet believed that the attack had really happened. To see the fleet destroyed before one's eyes on a peaceful Sunday morning defied credibility.

There was near-hysteria among some members of the

staff. What should they do now that they were at war—a war that wasn't supposed to have begun this way? In all the planning and the maneuvers, war was first declared, then the fighting began. The ships at Pearl would be loaded with ammunition and supplies, get up steam, and head out to sea, flags and pennants flying, with a navy band at the docks to send them on their way.

Rainbow 5 was obsolete. Perhaps in a year or two a new fleet with new battleships would lead American forces across the Pacific, but not now. There was no fleet left for a major offense, and barely enough for defense. And a Japanese fleet might be just over the horizon, ready to pour troops into Hawaii. Admiral Stark, chief of naval operations, radioed Kimmel that he expected the Japanese to attempt landings on Midway and the islands of Maui and Hawaii before coming ashore on Oahu. Reports from Wake told of heavy bombings, and the staff agreed there was no reason to capture Wake except to use it as a forward staging base for attacks against the Hawaiian Islands.

On December 8 (Hawaii time), Kimmel received an amended war plan from Washington. The new mission of the Pacific Fleet would be defensive—protect Hawaii, Wake, Johnston, and Palmyra Islands and the shipping lanes to Australia, and keep the enemy out of the Western Hemisphere. Kimmel and his staff began to draw together their meager war machinery to see what could be done about Wake.

There was no question of sending a major force of marines to reinforce Wake, because no major force was available in Hawaii that could be spared. They had 102 officers and 1,861 men (not including flying personnel), and few of those could be allocated to Wake, since all the islands needed more men. Finally it was decided that a force of fewer than 200 marines could be spared for Wake.

The next priority was fighter planes. The carrier *Saratoga* was steaming at maximum speed from San Diego to Pearl Harbor transporting another fighter squadron for Wake, VMF-221 with eighteen outdated Brewster Buffaloes. The essential radar equipment was located and set aside for shipment to Wake.

By December 9, Kimmel had formulated the basic plan for Wake's relief. He established Task Force 14, consisting of the *Saratoga*, three heavy cruisers—*Astoria, Minneapolis,* and *San Francisco*—nine destroyers, the fleet oiler *Neches,* and the *Tangier,* a seaplane tender converted to troop transport.

To divert the Japanese from this force, Task Force 11—a fleet of similar size but without transports, and including the carrier *Lexington*—was ordered to strike enemy bases at Jaluit, 800 miles south of Wake. A third force built around the carrier *Enterprise,* commanded by Vice Admiral Halsey, would operate in an area west of Johnston Island.

On December 10, marines of the Fourth Defense Battalion, still holding the positions they had set up at the Navy Yard during the Pearl Harbor attack, were alerted to be ready to embark. No one told them where they were going, but the men knew; there was only one place marines were needed urgently as far as they were concerned, and that was Wake.

Weapons and equipment were checked, new field uniforms issued, and the men given something they had never seen before—thin metal identification tags to be worn around their necks. The "dogtags" felt as strange as the new-style steel helmets issued three days before. They worked all day to get themselves and their equipment ready, but they did it eagerly. Fellow marines were in trouble, and the Fourth Defense Battalion was going to help them out. "We're headed for Wake," was the cry.

Late that night they received bad news. They were

told to stop their preparations and return to their positions around the Navy Yard. The expedition was called off. Anger and frustration ran deep.

Actually the expedition had not been called off, but it had been delayed for two reasons. First, the *Saratoga* needed several more days to get to Pearl Harbor, and second, Kimmel's staff wanted to make a new study of the entire Pacific situation. The marines on Wake would have to hold out on their own for a while longer.

The mood was quite different at the headquarters of Admiral Inouye and his staff at Truk during those first few days of war. The situation could not have been better for them. Everything was proceeding as planned for the Japanese as a whole and for Inouye's theater of operations as well. The reports from Tokyo on the complete surprise and extensive destruction at Pearl Harbor were cause for joyous celebration the night of December 8 (Wake time).

Inouye's own part of the war began that same day. He was charged with the capture of Wake and Guam from the Americans, and Makin and Tarawa, which were lightly held by the British. Attacks against all four islands commenced at once. Guam fell on the evening of the tenth, and Makin a few hours earlier; Tarawa was raided by a landing party which took several prisoners and left, there being nothing of value.

Only Wake remained, and Inouye was not as certain as Tokyo that it would be a minor operation. Inouye knew that Wake's defenses were well under way and that it was held by a larger enemy force than his other island targets. He believed there were 1,000 marines on Wake plus 600 construction workers. Also, while his pilots reported extensive damage to Wake's fortifications during their first raid, there were still four American planes in the air which had been very aggressive against the Japanese bombers. The flak too was heavy, and even if not very accurate, it had scored a number of hits.

Inouye would have liked to bomb the island for several more days before invading, but the timetable from Tokyo was clear: troops will land on December 11. The capture of Wake was entrusted to Rear Admiral Sadamichi Kajioka, commanding Destroyer Squadron 6, led by the new light cruiser *Yubari*. His task force consisted of the *Yubari*, two outdated light cruisers, six destroyers, two small destroyers outfitted as transports, two new transports, and two submarines. The operation was not deemed large enough to require an aircraft carrier.

Strangely enough, Inouye and Kajioka faced the same problem in regard to Wake as did Kimmel and his staff—not enough ships or men. Wake was a low priority mission for the Japanese and could not compete with the larger operations in the Philippines and Malaya. The Imperial Fourth Fleet had to make do with the forces it could scrape together.

A landing force of 450 men boarded the transports. It was planned that 150 would land on Wilkes Island and the rest would rush the beaches of Wake Island. Kajioka recognized the weakness of his force—"We expected to have a rough time," he wrote—and he was prepared to use the crews of his six destroyers as assault troops should the need arise.

The ships arrived at Roi-Namur from Truk on December 3, and sailed for Wake by a very circuitous route six days later. Although Kajioka did not expect to meet any enemy ships, he nevertheless screened his main force. The two submarines scouted seventy-five miles ahead and were instructed to be on the lookout for PT boats, of which Kajioka was very wary, around Wake. Ten miles ahead of the force, a lone destroyer searched the sea for American ships.

Admiral Kajioka was relieved when the weather turned bad south of Wake. He was sure now that he would not be detected. At 3:00 A.M. on December 11, lookouts reported Wake Island on the horizon. The rain had stopped, but the wind was still strong and the sea rough. The ships moved in closer, and lookouts peered through night binoculars for any sign of activity. Nothing was moving on the island, and Kajioka concluded that he had caught the marines by surprise. His troops were readied, and with the *Yubari* in the lead the task force began its approach to bombardment stations off the south coast of Wake.

Two marine lookouts on the south beach of Wake were the first to spot the Japanese fleet. They looked, discussed it for a moment, then looked again. They didn't want to raise a false alarm and wake up Major Devereux for nothing, but the more they watched, the more convinced they were that there was movement out there. It was not quite 3:00 A.M. when they cranked their field telephone and rang the command post.

Corporal Robert McC. Brown had telephone watch duty that night in the command post, and when the lookouts reported, he nudged Devereux, who immediately took the phone.

"What kind of movement?" he asked.

"Just something seemed to be moving, sir. Then we couldn't see it anymore. I'm not sure but I think we saw a faint blink of light, too."

Devereux told Corporal Brown to call all the other posts to ask if they had seen anything. He waited for their replies, pondering what to do. Maybe nothing was out there—just tricks played on tired eyes in the light of the half-moon. Perhaps one of the American submarines patrolling around the island had surfaced to recharge its batteries. Devereux didn't want to wake the garrison unless he was convinced it was the enemy. His men were dead tired; they needed every minute of sleep they were allowed.

Corporal Brown's voice intruded on his thoughts. An

observation post at the end of Wake near the boat channel said they saw "some sort of movement" off the south coast.

"Did they see any lights?" Devereux asked.

"No, sir, no lights," Brown said. "Whatever it was, was quite a ways off."

Captain Wesley M. Platt, commander of the detachment on Wilkes Island, called in.

"It sure looks like there are some ships out there," he said.

Devereux had to see for himself. With his runner, he went down to the beach close to the boat channel. He trained his powerful night binoculars out to sea and systematically scanned the water. Slowly his glasses moved across the horizon. Suddenly they stopped.

"Well," he said in a quiet voice, "there they are."

He saw little more than blurs, dark vague shapes a shade darker than the surrounding water and sky. An untrained observer would not have noticed them, but Devereux knew right away that they were ships—and he knew they were not American.

He returned to the command post and ordered the garrison to battle stations. He issued all orders by phone; there would be no ringing bugles to alert the enemy.

When all the guns were manned and ready, Devereux had only one command: "Hold your fire until I give the word."

No one knew how large the enemy force was. It was still too far offshore to identify the numbers or kinds of ships. But Devereux thought the force looked sizable enough to have ships with guns larger than his, and that meant that the enemy could stand out to sea beyond the range of his five-inch batteries and pound the tiny atoll into submission.

He knew there was only one chance for Wake's survival, and it was slim. If the marines could draw the ships in close enough for the five-inch guns to open up, perhaps they could do some real damage to the enemy force. And the only way to draw them in was to let the enemy think that they had caught the defenders by surprise and that their bombing raids had destroyed the islands' big guns. It would mean a long, frustrating wait for the marines on Wake, watching the ships get closer and closer and not doing anything about it, but Devereux believed the tactic could work.

He notified Commander Cunningham, then called Major Putnam at the airfield.

"How many planes can you send up, Paul?"

"Four," was the terse answer.

"When will it be light enough to send them up?"

"Not until a half hour before daylight."

"Don't take off until I open fire," Devereux said. "I'm trying to draw them in and the planes would give the show away."

"Okay," Putnam said. "Good luck."

The big question, which neither one asked, was how many planes the enemy had. It was inconceivable that they might not have any, that there was not a carrier lurking somewhere beyond the horizon. Major Putnam's four-plane air force could be in for a lot of trouble.

The Japanese ships closed on Wake with great caution. They were having problems getting the landing force from the transports into the invasion barges. The sea was still rough and the winds strong, and the light landing craft bobbed and heaved in the water. A few of them overturned.

On Wake the time dragged by with agonizing slowness. All eyes watched the ships approach the beaches, and the tension mounted by the minute. The men kept their thoughts to themselves. They knew it was an invasion attempt. In an hour or so heavy shells would come screaming in at them, and Japanese troops would swarm across the beaches. They knew that Guam had already fallen. Would Wake be next?

Major Devereux stood by the entrance to his command post watching the ships. Four A.M. passed, then 4:30, and the defenders of Wake waited, watching the ships come nearer.

By 5:00 there was sufficient daylight for Devereux to identify the Japanese task force. When he saw the two light cruisers, he knew for sure that he was outgunned. His five-inchers were no match for their six-inch guns. It confirmed his strategy; Wake's only hope was to draw the enemy within range of his five-inch guns.

He reached for the phone and cautioned the gun commanders again.

"Under no circumstances fire until I give the word."

The cruiser *Yubari,* with Admiral Kajioka aboard, was now 8,000 yards south of Peacock Point. He ordered the helmsman to turn the ship to port and begin a run westward paralleling Wake's south coast. The rest of the task force ran the same course about 1,000 yards out beyond the *Yubari.*

On Peacock Point, the five-inch battery commander, First Lieutenant Clarence A. Barninger, removed the camouflage from around his guns, reasoning that the higher ground behind his position would prevent the enemy from seeing them in the dim early morning light. His gunners began to track the cruiser, the long barrels swinging slowly in time with the cruiser's speed. Anxious hands rested on the firing triggers waiting for the command to open up.

At 5:30 the *Yubari* commenced firing and continued doing so during the rest of its westward run. A few minutes later, the other two cruisers opened fire. High velocity shells fell along the beach and in the vicinity of Camp 1. Diesel oil tanks were set ablaze and riflemen and machine gunners hugged the ground in their dugouts. At the gun batteries, marines were growing angry at not being allowed to return the fire. Some gunners cursed aloud as they watched the Japanese ships cruise by them unmolested.

The *Yubari* completed its westward run off Wake's south shore and reversed course, joined by the two destroyer-transports. They had to turn toward the island to do so, and when they completed the turn and began to steam eastward, it was at a distance of 6,000 yards. Meanwhile, other ships steamed close to the western end of Wilkes Island. It was now past 6:00 A.M., and the ships were plainly visible in the bright morning light.

The phone in Devereux's command post kept ringing as anxious battery commanders begged for permission to open fire. Corporal Brown automatically repeated the same message: "Hold your fire till the major gives the word."

Two batteries were now trained on the two separate groups of ships: Battery A at Peacock Point and Battery L on Wilkes, commanded by Second Lieutenant John A. McAlister. Both batteries lacked proper fire-control equipment, and McAlister's guns did not even have a range finder. He could only guess at the range; there was no way to determine it accurately.

More shells exploded on the island, and the nearest ship was now less than 5,000 yards offshore.

The gunners were growing furious. In Battery A, a sergeant yelled to no one in particular, "What does that dumb little bastard want us to do? Let 'em run over us without even spitting back?" The *Yubari* was now 4,500 yards away from Battery A.

At 6:10 Devereux spoke calmly into the field telephone.

"Commence firing."

The big guns exploded instantly. Lieutenant Barninger's first salvo from Battery A went over the *Yubari*, sending up two great columns of water beyond the ship.

The cruiser immediately heeled over in a tight turn and began to race away from Wake on a zigzag course. Barninger stood out in the open on the roof of his command post directing the fire. He ordered the range lowered by 500 yards, but before he could fire again, shells from the cruiser fell nearby. Shrapnel clattered against the sides of the hut he was perched on, but he made no move to take cover. He had only one thing on his mind: get the cruiser.

An artillery duel followed. Each side came close, but neither scored a hit. Meanwhile, the cruiser was picking up speed and getting further away. Spouts of water straddled the ship. Then, at a distance of 5,700 yards, shells from both guns struck the *Yubari* amidships, just above the waterline. Smoke and steam poured out through the holes, and the ship lost speed.

At 7,000 yards she was hit again, almost at the same point. Smoke engulfed the whole side of the ship, and she turned to starboard to try to hide in her own smoke. A destroyer rushed in between the *Yubari* and the atoll to lay down a smoke screen, but it was immediately hit in the forecastle by a lucky miss that had been aimed at the cruiser. It turned sharply and raced away.

The cruiser continued to steam away, and Battery A scored another hit on the forward turret before she moved out of range. The gunners saw the *Yubari*, enveloped by smoke, creep away, stop, and then continue. All the while she continued to fire at the battery position but inflicted only one casualty—a marine who was slightly wounded.

At the same time, Battery L on Wilkes had more than its share of targets. Facing Wilkes were three destroyers, two transports, and two light cruisers which had broken away from the *Yubari* before Battery A had started to fire.

The lead destroyer was only 4,500 yards offshore when Lieutenant McAlister began firing. He guessed the range, and his first two salvos went over the destroyer, but the third salvo hit it with both shells. There was a spectacular explosion, and for a moment the ship was covered with smoke and falling water. As the smoke cleared, the gunners could see that the ship had broken in two and was sinking. In less than two minutes it was gone. Wake had sunk its first ship.

The men of Battery L went wild with excitement. They shouted and pounded each other on the back, oblivious to the other enemy targets. An old China hand, Platoon Sergeant Henry Bedell, put his hands on his hips and yelled in a voice that overrode the noise of the surf, "Knock it off, you bastards, and get back on the guns! What d'y' think this is, a ball game?" After the battle, one of his men said, "No wonder the Japs took off—they thought Bedell was yelling at them."

The task force was scattering in all directions, each ship zigzagging frantically to get out of the range of fire. Destroyers threw out heavy smoke screens for protection. Battery L got one hit on another destroyer before the smoke concealed it. They fired several more salvos until the smoke became so thick that McAlister could no longer see where his shells were landing.

Enemy fire hit all around the battery, and they suddenly found themselves out of ammunition. The gunners raced to the magazines for a fresh supply and quickly opened fire again on a transport. They hit it once; then it disappeared behind a freshly laid smoke screen. McAlister then trained his guns on a cruiser some 9,000 yards offshore, hitting it in the aft end. The ship turned away, trailing thick smoke.

Now it was the turn of Battery B at Peale Island's Toki Point. Under the command of First Lieutenant Woodrow M. Kessler, the guns opened fire on a force of three destroyers at a range of 10,000 yards. The destroyers returned a heavy and accurate fire perilously

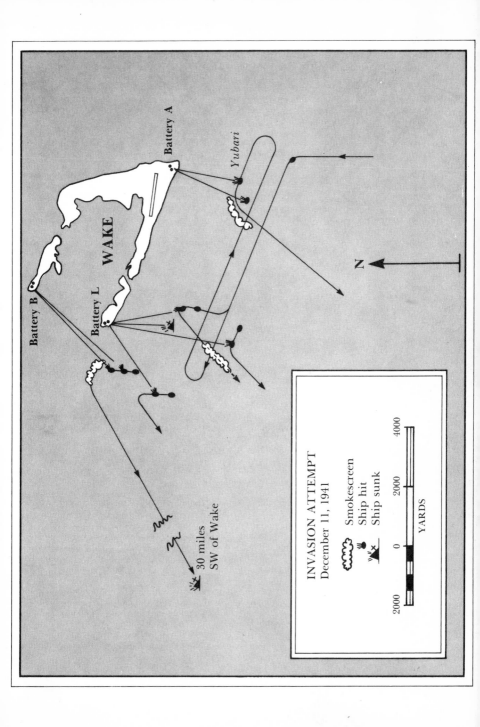

INVASION ATTEMPT
December 11, 1941

Smokescreen
Ship hit
Ship sunk

YARDS
2000 0 2000 4000

WAKE

Battery A

Battery L

Battery B

Yubari

30 miles
SW of Wake

N

close to the guns, knocking out their communications with the command post. Then a recoil cylinder plug on Battery B's number 2 gun blew out, injuring Corporal A. F. Terry in the side and disabling the gun. Terry refused first aid, and he and his crew raced to the other gun to serve as ammunition carriers so that a steadier rate of fire could be maintained. After firing ten salvos, the gun hit the lead destroyer. The second ship in line laid down a smoke screen, and the three ships slipped away.

At 7:00 A.M., Admiral Kajioka ordered all ships to withdraw and Devereux told his gunners to cease firing.

At the moment Wake's guns had begun firing, 6:10 A.M., the four Wildcats had taken off, piloted by Major Putnam and Captains Henry T. Elrod, Herbert C. Freuler, and Frank C. Tharin. They climbed swiftly to 12,000 feet and made a thorough search of the waters beyond Wake for an enemy aircraft carrier. When they were convinced there wasn't one, they returned to do battle with the Japanese task force, which by that time was already steaming away from Wake.

They located the ships about fifteen miles southwest of the atoll and bore in to attack with machine gun fire and the hundred-pound bombs hanging beneath the wings in their improvised bomb racks. They dove straight through the heavy flak, dropped their bombs, and headed back to Wake for another load. They flew a total of ten sorties that morning, dropped twenty bombs, and fired 20,000 rounds of .50 caliber machine gun bullets. Each time they returned to Wake, mechanics counted more and more flak holes in the wings, but back they went to do battle.

The fighters scored hits on both light cruisers. One of the transports was hit in the stern by a bomb which started a giant gasoline fire. At about 7:30, a destroyer they had hit on an earlier sortie suddenly blew up with a tremendous explosion and sank. The planes also damaged one of the destroyer-transports.

It was a gratifying success for the pilots of VMF-211, but it cost them dearly. All the planes suffered flak damage, and the main fuel line in Captain Elrod's plane had been cut. With his engine sputtering, he turned and headed for Wake, losing altitude rapidly. The marines watched his plane wobble and lurch through the sky. He was approaching the island but falling so fast that it looked as though he would crash in the sea. Still he flew, almost on the water. Elrod nursed the plane along and made land by a margin of a few feet, crash-landing on the beach. Putnam, Devereux, and others raced to the wreckage and pulled him out. Amazingly he was uninjured—not even a scratch—but the plane was a total loss. There would be no reclaiming it.

"Honest, I'm sorry as hell about the plane," Elrod said.

Meanwhile, another plane was in trouble. Captain Freuler limped back to Wake with his plane's oil line shot away and bullet holes through the air cleaner and one cylinder of the engine. The engine cut out just short of the field, but he had sufficient altitude to make it, coming in for a perfect landing. The plane itself was all right, but the engine had been damaged beyond repair.

Half of Wake's air force was now disabled, but the enemy's losses were much higher. Two ships had been sunk and seven damaged. The Japanese later admitted to losses of 500 men, but postwar American estimates placed the casualties closer to 700. On Wake Island, four marines were slightly wounded; there were no deaths. It was an amazing victory—the odds had certainly been against them in the beginning.

After the planes were all back and the columns of smoke could no longer be seen in the distance, Corporal Brown turned to Major Devereux and said, "It's been quite a day, Major, hasn't it?"

But there was more to come. After Major Putnam and Captain Tharin had landed, it was time for the planes to take off again for the Combat Air Patrol. Lieutenants Davidson and Kinney were at the controls this time, both eager for more victories. They soon had their chance. At 10:00 they spotted a force of thirty bombers coming in from the northeast at 18,000 feet. The Wildcats tore into the formation with all guns blazing. Within minutes two bombers spun wildly into the sea, and a third, trailing heavy smoke, turned away from the formation and headed back to the Japanese base.

As the planes came over the atoll, the antiaircraft batteries on Wake and Peale opened up, splattering the formation with well over 200 rounds. One plane caught fire and wobbled out of control, and the gunners cheered as they watched it nose-dive into the sea off Wilkes Island. Three other bombers were hit and left clouds of black smoke.

On the ground, Gunner Hamas and a crew of six civilians were waiting to cross from Wake to Wilkes with a truckload of vital shells and powder for the five-inch battery. Hamas drove the truck onto the small ferry, and it pulled away from the dock just as the raid started. Hamas and Boatswain's Mate Second Class Kirby Ludwick, the boat's pilot, heard the first bombs fall in the distance. They knew that one hit would blow them all sky-high, but they shrugged and continued their slow passage across the channel—and they made it.

It was the enemy's least effective raid to date, causing no casualties and only minor physical damage. The marines and the civilians had learned well their lessons in how to survive.

The raid did, however, lead to another tedious and difficult gun-moving detail. Some of the bombs had fallen perilously close to Battery D at Toki Point on Peale Island, and Devereux concluded that the battery had been located and would be a prime target in the next raid. There was no choice but to move it, though it meant another long, sleepless night for the men assigned to the job.

At 5:00 that afternoon, just before the men assembled to do the job, they sighted a smoke bomb and a chain flare of three bright red balls about two miles off Toki Point. The same signal occurred twice during the next twenty minutes, then died away. It was too dark to send a plane up to investigate, and the Wake defenders never learned what the mysterious signals meant. There was a great deal of speculation about them, and most men thought the flares had been sent up by survivors of the day's invasion attempt or the bombing raid who were adrift in the sea.

After darkness fell, a somber ceremony took place— the burial of those killed since the first day of war. There had not been time before; bomb shelters and defenses for the living had to take precedence. A civilian construction worker operated the large, noisy dragline and scooped out a long trench to serve as a common grave. Individual graves were ruled out because they would tell the enemy how many casualties the island had suffered.

Trucks brought the dead from the reefers where they had been stored, and the sheet-wrapped bodies were laid side by side in the trench. Civilian and military were buried together—more than seventy men. The burial party was small; most of the men couldn't be relieved from their posts to attend. Devereux, Cunningham, and Teters were there, along with the father of one of the civilian dead and four marines from the nearest machine gun emplacement who formed the firing squad.

There was no military chaplain on Wake, but one of the civilian workers, bearded John O'Neal, was a Mormon lay preacher who quietly had visited foxhole after foxhole during the raids to offer comfort and support. He said a short prayer, the four marines fired their rifles in a last salute, and a bulldozer quickly filled in the trench. Then the area was camouflaged and everyone went back to work.

After the ceremony, Commander Cunningham ordered that there be no more mass burials. From then on, he said, casualties would be buried where they fell or in the nearest convenient spot. One man was already buried where he had been killed. Private John Katchak, nineteen years old, was the first member of the marine defense battalion to die. A bomb had fallen on the edge of his foxhole and turned it into his grave. His buddies built up a small mound over what had been the foxhole and placed some chunks of coral on it. When they finished, they gathered around and quietly murmured the Lord's Prayer.

Commander Cunningham received several messages from Pearl Harbor that day. One ordered him to locate and destroy a confidential publication dealing with the range finder equipment Pan American had been using. It was an easy order to comply with. The Japanese had already taken care of it by totally destroying the Pan Am headquarters.

Another message congratulated them for having beaten off the invasion attempt. Those on Wake, the communique said, had performed their duties "in accordance with the highest traditions of the Naval Service." Earlier in the day, Cunningham had sent a report to Pearl Harbor on the battle and the extent of enemy losses, and in so doing he was inadvertently responsible for the greatest myth that developed about Wake Island.

After he had written his report, it was put into code before it was transmitted. In 1941, standard operating procedure called for padding messages at the beginning and the end with material that was patently nonsense. Cunningham's report was sent out by his decoder, prefaced by the following:

"SEND US STOP NOW IS THE TIME FOR ALL

GOOD MEN TO COME TO THE AID OF THEIR
PARTY STOP CUNNINGHAM MORE JAPS . . ."

Someone in Honolulu seized upon the opening and
closing words of the padding, and a propaganda legend
was born. It grew more complicated in its invisible path
to the American people and became one of the most
popular stories of that early part of the war.

A few days later, the defenders of Wake were angered
when they heard stateside announcers proclaim Wake's
gesture of defiance. Pearl Harbor, it was said, had asked
Wake if there was anything it needed, and the answer
had flashed back: "Yes, send us more Japs!" That was
the one thing Wake's marines didn't need, and it was the
only thing they were destined to get.

A large party of marines, with the help of more than
one hundred civilians, went to work moving Battery D
from Toki Point all the way to the other end of Peale
Island. As they started to dismantle the position, they
discovered that nearly all the sandbags encircling the
guns had been riddled with shrapnel and were useless.
It was a shortage that plagued every gun position, and
they took to using paper cement bags and empty ammunition boxes. This was what Wake needed—materiel
and equipment—sandbags, firing pins, recoil fluid,
range finders, planes, and spare parts.

As Major Devereux watched his exhausted marines
filling cement bags with sand, he wondered about the
possibility of being reinforced before the Japanese returned to avenge the morning's defeat. Then he remembered an old Marine Corps axiom he had first
heard as a private.

"Maybe you oughta get more, maybe you will get
more, but all you can depend on getting is what you already got."

By then, the end of the fourth day of war, Devereux
knew well the truth of that.

At 4:45 the next morning, the antiaircraft guns were

finally set up in their new positions and camouflaged, and the men dragged themselves off to catch a few hours of sleep before the next raid.

But the enemy surprised them. The next raid was only fifteen minutes away.

Aerial view of Wake Island.
Navy Department photo, National Archives.

Commander Winfield Scott Cunningham,
taken in 1937.
Navy Department photo, National Archives.

Major James Devereux, taken in 1945 after his release from a Japanese POW camp.
U.S. Marine Corps photo.

Pan American Clipper at the Wake Island dock.
Courtesy of Pan American World Airways, Inc.

Major Paul Putnam; photo released in 1942.
Navy Department photo, National Archives.

Grumman F4F-3 Wildcat fighter plane.
U.S. Marine Corps photo.

Aerial view of the civilian construction workers' barracks on Wake Island, taken from an
attacking Japanese plane.
U.S. Marine Corps photo.

Painting of the defense of Wake Island, by
Albin Henning.
U.S. Marine Corps photo.

Cartoon: "To the Glory of a Scar Spangled
Banner."
U.S. Marine Corps photo.

7 JAP WARSHIPS
1 CRUISER
4 DESTROYERS
1 SUBMARINE
1 GUNBOAT
9 JAP PLANES

WAKE

Cartoon: "Semper Fidelis," by Jerry Doyle.
U.S. Marine Corps photo.

Wreckage of one of the Wake Island Wildcat
fighters.
Navy Department photo, National Archives.

Painting: "Remember Wake Island," by Private First Class James Pearl, U.S. Army.
U.S. Marine Corps photo.

Colonel Walter Bayler returns to Wake Island in September, 1945. The last man off Wake Island in 1941, Bayler was the first American to return.
U.S. Marine Corps photo.

Japanese examining F4F in its covered revetment.
U.S. Marine Corps photo.

Wake Island prisoners aboard ship on their way to POW camps. Reproduced from *Freedom*, an English-language propaganda magazine published by the Japanese. Commander Cunningham, in dress uniform, is seated. Dan Teters, civilian construction chief, is seated next to Cunningham. Behind Teters stands Lieutenant Gustav Kahn, the navy doctor. To Kahn's right is Commander Campbell Keene, in charge of the patrol plane facility.
Courtesy of Wide World Photos, Inc. (Associated Press).

The formal surrender ceremony on Wake Island, September 4, 1945. Brigadier General Lawson H. M. Sanderson, Commanding General of the Fourth Marine Air Wing, is in the forefront. Second from the left, behind General Sanderson, is Colonel Bayler.
U.S. MARINE Corps photo.

A Marine pays silent tribute to an unidentified American killed in the fighting on Wake Island.
U.S. Marine Corps photo.

The Wake Island Memorial dedicated to "Captain Henry T. Elrod and the gallant defenders of Wake." The propeller and engine cowling are from F4F No. 9, Captain Elrod's plane, which crash-landed on the beach. The monument was built by Lieutenant Marshall K. Phillips, U.S. Coast Guard, in 1955. The cowling is now on a restored Wildcat in the National Air and Space Museum in Washington, D.C.
U.S. Marine Corps photo.

6

"When Time Stood Still"

With the dawning of December 12, the battle for Wake entered a new phase which Commander Cunningham described as a time of "attrition." Major Devereux called it the period "when time stood still." The memories of the Wake survivors, when they wrote their reports after the war, were sharp and clear for the first four days of the battle and again for the last two or three days, but they found it difficult to remember exactly what had happened during the middle phase.

Major Devereux wrote: "In between was this foggy blur of days and nights when time stood still. . . . the only certain memory is how much you wanted a whole night's sleep. . . . the days blurred together in a dreary sameness of bombing and endless work and always that aching need for sleep. I have seen men standing with their eyes open, staring at nothing, and they did not hear me when I spoke to them. They were out on their feet. They became so punch drunk from weariness that frequently a man would forget an order almost as soon as he turned away. He would have to come back later and ask what you wanted him to do, and sometimes it was hard for you to remember."

Thoughts narrowed to the moment. Memories of

home and family grew distant and confused; they belonged to another life, one that had no bearing on today. To many men, there was no longer any life beyond that tiny atoll. Their existence began there and, as far as they knew, it would end there. There was no world but sand and coral, falling bombs, explosions, work, and the constant need for sleep. And each day was worse as the fatigue accumulated and drained more of their energy. Major Devereux's longest stretch of uninterrupted sleep during that period was two hours.

With the bone-numbing fatigue came boredom. Commander Cunningham wrote: "We waited. We spent hours, even days, in waiting. Then the planes flew over, the bombs fell, we made the repairs that could be made, and the waiting began all over again. . . . There was simply nothing to do the majority of time but wait."

And the rats became more troublesome. Disturbed by the bombings, they swarmed in droves into foxholes and shelters, interrupting what little rest was to be had. During one raid, a large rat went berserk and began running in circles faster and faster. Suddenly it leaped into a foxhole and attacked the luckless marine who was in it. The rat clamped its teeth on the man's nose and hung on until it was beaten to death.

The birds were also made more desperate by the raids. They squawked and flew and ran around wildly. Tired men sometimes mistook them for planes. After heavy raids the islands were littered with hundreds of dead birds killed by concussion. In addition to their other duties, the men had to dispose of the dead birds as a sanitary measure.

Then diarrhea struck. Scores of men tried to carry on in spite of it, but they grew so weak they had to be carried to the hospital. The marines and the civilians who worked with them were careful about their waste and garbage, but the civilians hiding out in the brush took no such precautions, and flies carried disease from one end of the atoll to the other, disabling men as effectively as shrapnel.

Still they waited and endured. They moved mechanically, automatically from foxhole to gun and back again, always watching the sky for more planes. They listened on their shortwave sets to music from another world, Honolulu and San Francisco. They swore at silken-voiced announcers who told them the only thing the marines on Wake wanted was "more Japs," and what an inspiration they were to the American people, and how the factories were gearing up to produce 10,000 planes, a thousand ships. And they saw the remains of their air force, the worn-out guns and equipment, and they wondered if any of those shiny new airplanes and ships would get to them in time.

"Give us ten new planes," they said, "even five. Give us something!"

But most of all they wanted sleep. The days passed, but time on Wake Island stood still.

On the thirteenth of December, Admiral Kajioka's battered task force limped into the harbor at Kwajalein. Admiral Inouye's earlier concern, his staff now realized, had been well founded; Wake was not going to be an easy victory. Indeed, it might not be a victory at all, for the longer Wake held out, the greater the chances of it being reinforced. It was out of the question, of course, that Wake should remain in American hands; it was too close to vital Japanese positions. It was a breach in the wall the Japanese were building across the central Pacific, and it had to be taken soon.

Workmen at Kwajalein swarmed over the battle-scarred ships, and navy staff officers analyzed the defeat and prepared a new attack. Rear Admiral Marushige Kuninori, in command of the two damaged light cruisers, laid the blame for their failure on four factors: vigorous and active fire from Wake's coastal artillery; aggressive, courageous, and skillful American fighter pilots; bad weather; and an attacking force that was too small.

The planners decided that the only one of these factors they could influence was the last, so they set about enlarging the size of their force. Admiral Inouye assigned two replacement destroyers, sister ships of the two that had been sunk, and a larger and more powerful destroyer that mounted six five-inch guns. A mine layer in the Marianas was ordered to pick up the men of the Maizuru Second Special Landing Force on Saipan and bring them to Roi-Namur, where they would become a part of the amphibious assault force. Another transport and a seaplane tender were also added to the fleet.

The troops rehearsed their mission on December 15, while Inouye's superiors at Combined Fleet Headquarters reordered the priorities of their mid-Pacific strategy and diverted a carrier task force to the Wake operation. With the addition of this force (two carriers, four old heavy cruisers, two new heavy cruisers, and six destroyers) to the existing units, Wake was clearly no longer a low-priority target in Japan's program of conquest. Rear Admiral Hiroaki Abe was placed in overall command of the task force, with Admiral Kajioka in charge of its amphibious portion.

With this considerable fleet, the staff laid out a program for Wake's capture which was little more than an elaboration of the original plan, with one major difference. This time, more attention would be paid to the systematic destruction of Wake's defenses prior to landing troops. For the two days preceding the invasion, the planes of the two carriers would pound Wake with raid after raid, concentrating on the fighter planes, antiaircraft and coastal batteries, and the machine gun emplacements.

In order to avoid any of Wake's accurate five-inch guns which might remain in operation, the invasion was

scheduled to take place during the last hours of darkness before dawn. To ensure surprise, there would be
no naval bombardment. Troops would be put ashore as
quickly as possible by running the two destroyer-transports aground on the south shore close to the airfield.
In addition, landing barges carrying fifty men each
would land at other points on Wake and Wilkes Islands.
In all, 1,000 Special Naval Landing Force troops would
swarm ashore. And if they were not enough, a 500-man
reserve from the ships' crews could be thrown into the
battle.

There was no turning back this time, no retreat.
There was an almost desperate quality about this second
attack. Perhaps the Japanese realized that if they failed
this time, there might not be another chance. Whatever
the reason, their determination to win was made clear by
the final part of their invasion plan: if the 1,000-man
landing force was not enough, and if the 500-man reserve force was still not sufficient, the destroyers were
ordered to run for the shore and beach themselves so
their crews could join the battle.

The invasion was set for December 23.

The marines at Pearl Harbor had been seething with
frustration since the relief expedition was called off on
December 10. When they heard the news of the re-
treating Japanese invasion force, they were all the more
eager to get to Wake. Sitting in dugouts around the
Navy Yard, faced with the evidence of America's shattering defeat, the marines wanted to get into action.
Guam had fallen, and Wake could be next. The
Japanese would return; if help was not sent, it would be
only a question of time before Wake fell and more
marines became prisoners of war. But for now, Wake
was fighting back and winning, and it was the only place
where Americans were doing that. The marines of the
aborted relief force wanted to be a part of it. They were

not alone—the detachment of marines of the U.S.S. *Washington* had volunteered to be flown to Wake Island.

Early on the morning of December 12 (December 13 on Wake), the good news came—new orders to embark. As before, the men were not told where they were going, but no one had to tell them. They knew. With great excitement they packed up their gear and marched down to the dock to board the U.S.S. *Tangier,* a seaplane tender temporarily converted to carry troops and cargo.

All that day, equipment and stores were loaded on the *Tangier.* One of the few radar sets in the entire Pacific was carefully lashed down on the ship's small flight deck. Fire-control equipment for the three-inch and five-inch guns was brought aboard, along with millions of rounds of machine gun ammunition and 9,000 rounds of five-inch shells. In addition, 12,000 rounds of the latest type of three-inch antiaircraft shells with new thirty-second time fuses were loaded—the entire supply available in Pearl Harbor. Suddenly it was discovered that no one had trajectory charts or firing tables for the shells, so new were they. Frantic officers raced from one ack-ack battery to another and finally located one copy in the possession of an army officer at Fort Shafter who agreed to donate it to the marines.

As the loading proceeded, other marines in the area of Pearl Harbor got word of the relief force and came down to the dock to see their comrades on the *Tangier.*

"Goodby and give 'em Hell!" they yelled.

The period of attrition on Wake began at 5:00 A.M. on December 12. Two four-engine Japanese patrol planes roared in over the island. They bombed and strafed Wake and Peale and shot up the airstrip but caused no casualties. Above the planes, Captain Tharin's Wildcat was cruising alone. He dove on one of the planes, and his guns riddled its wings. Desperately the seaplane twisted and turned, but Tharin hung on its tail, methodically cutting the ship to pieces. He chased it out to sea and watched it disintegrate as it slammed into the water.

To everyone's amazement, there was no midday raid on the twelfth. The appointed time came and went, and no bomber formation appeared. In a strange way, it was a handicap. On the other days the men had known that by 10:00 or 11:00 in the morning the big raid of the day was over; they knew they had survived again and would not have to face a bombing for twenty-four hours. But on the twelfth, noon appeared, then 1:00, and still no planes came. It was disquieting. They waited and watched the sky to the south, but it was empty.

That afternoon the marines tested a new device, a homemade sound locator. They desperately needed something that would detect the sound of approaching aircraft amidst the constant noise of the surf. Though it had not happened since the first day, the Japanese could still sneak up on them using a rain squall for cover and be overhead before anybody on the ground saw or heard them.

For some time, a small group had tried to work out the mathematical properties of a listening horn that would trap every decibel of aircraft engine noise while excluding the noise of the surf. The finished product was a crude pyramidal box with flat plywood sides. They tried it out on their own planes as they came in from patrol, but it failed. It was worse than listening with their own ears—it magnified the sound of the surf! Improvisation could only go so far.

Another group of mechanically minded marines and civilians was also hard at work, and its efforts produced more positive results. Kinney and Hamilton and their willing helpers miraculously built—or created—a plane out of the wreckage of all the others. For a time, the Wake Island air force was boosted to three aircraft.

That evening all three took off for patrol, though one

was later than the others—which turned out to be quite a stroke of fortune. Lieutenant Kliewer's Wildcat refused to start; that particular plane was always hard to start. By the time he managed to take off, he was fifteen minutes behind the others. As he reached the altitude of the patrol and started after them, he saw something in the water about twenty-five miles offshore. He focused his binoculars on it and recognized it as a submarine—and it was not where the two American subs were known to be.

He maneuvered across the sky so that the sun was at his back and cut the Wildcat into a screaming dive from 10,000 feet. When he was close enough not to waste ammunition, he opened fire with his machine guns, and he didn't pull out until the last possible second. He released both bombs, and they exploded about fifteen feet from the sub. His plane was so low that fragments from the bombs tore holes in the wings and tail surfaces. By the time he pulled out of his dive and circled back, the submarine was gone, but a telltale patch of oil remained on the surface.* Lieutenant Kliewer could not know for sure if it had been sunk or merely submerged, but what happened the following day was proof enough to the men on Wake that the submarine had been sunk.

December 13 was noteworthy for the defenders of Wake. It was the first day without any air raid since the war began. The men of VMF-211 attributed this to the sinking of the submarine, which they believed had been providing radio homing signals which allowed the Japanese pilots to find that tiny spot in the ocean. The marine pilots knew how difficult it was to locate Wake, and the enemy had to fly almost 600 miles over water with no landmarks to aid in navigation.

---

* Postwar examination of Japanese records revealed that two of their submarines were lost some twenty-five miles southeast of the atoll during the battle for Wake. One was listed as lost to "disaster" and not to American action. The loss of the other sub was listed as "cause unknown." This was probably the one attacked by Kliewer.

Lieutenant Kinney wrote that the Japanese "always seemed to hit the island on the head just about the same time each day. Moreover, we heard a lot of funny radio signals. We never had any radio direction-finding equipment, and therefore couldn't take any bearings on these strange signals, but I am convinced that the sub was leading them in."

Whatever the reason, the men on Wake enjoyed their first quiet day, though most of it was spent, like the previous days, working on the atoll's defenses. But at least there was a chance for a little more sleep, and some men even took a swim in the lagoon, though always watchful of the southern sky.

Unfortunately there was also tragedy on that peaceful day. That evening as Captain Freuler started his takeoff for patrol, his plane suddenly swerved to the left toward a group of civilians and a large crane parked at the edge of the runway. Freuler tried desperately to straighten out, but he couldn't turn the plane. The civilians were scattering, but Freuler realized he would hit some of them—and the crane. At the last moment he was able to turn sharply and crash into the dense undergrowth. He climbed out unhurt, but the plane was smashed beyond repair. Kinney and Hamilton examined it and shook their heads sadly; even they could not reclaim this one. It was moved to the parking area and set up with all the other hopelessly wrecked planes which served as targets for enemy bombs.

As though to make up for a day without bombing, explosions rocked Wake at 3:30 the following morning, Sunday, December 14. Three four-engine flying boats roared over, dropped their bombs harmlessly around the airfield, and left, causing no damage but shortening the hours of sleep the weary men would get that day.

At 11:00 things turned considerably worse as thirty bombers came over—one of the heaviest raids so far. This time the Japanese concentrated on Camp 1 and the dugouts and shelters close to the shore of Wake Island. In his command post, Major Devereux and a group of marines waited silently under a roof of heavy timbers covered over with coral and sandbags, and they could hear the bombs get closer and closer. Their eight-foot-deep shelter shook violently and sand sifted down between cracks in the timbers. The whistling of the bombs sounded directly overhead, and in the corner of the dugout Corporal Brown was mumbling, his words muted by the explosions.

"What the hell are you doing, Brown?" someone yelled irritably.

"I'm praying, you God-damn fool!" Brown shouted back.

At that instant, the whole shelter seemed to rise in the air. A blast of flame shot across the entrance, and the room filled with smoke and clouds of sand. The concussion rocked men off their feet.

Close by at the airfield, men pressed themselves flat in their foxholes as explosions burst all around them. There was a shout from somewhere, and a few heads rose cautiously to see smoke cover one of the parked Wildcats. A bomb had fallen inside a revetment and turned the tail of the ship into a twisted, flaming aluminum skeleton.

Without hesitating a moment, Lieutenant Kinney, Sergeant Hamilton, and Aviation Machinist's Mate First Class James F. Hesson, one of the best mechanics around, raced toward the burning plane.* Flames reached upward and began creeping toward the fuel tank. The three men worked frantically at the nose of the ship to remove the engine and drag it away. That plane was a total loss, but the engine would fly again in a new plane cannibalized from parts of all the others.

The three-inch guns blazed away at the enemy planes.

---

* Hesson was later awarded the Navy Cross for his services to VMF-211.

Two bombers caught fire and plunged into the sea, but the others came on, never breaking formation. In the command post, men choked on the fumes and picked themselves up, amazed that they were still alive. But it wasn't over yet. A second V-formation of planes was overhead, and the ground shook once again, and more sand rained down on them. Then the third formation dropped their bombs, and there were more explosions. Finally it was quiet.

Inside the command post, "men looked at each other as though they could not quite comprehend," Major Devereux wrote, "and then it was like a great weight lifting from your chest. You wouldn't die today. Not this morning, anyhow."

The men filed outside the bunker and saw with horror how close one bomb had fallen—directly on a corner of the dugout. A foot or two more and it would have turned the command post into a crater—and a grave.

"We're sure gonna run out of luck quick," one man said, "if we keep using it up at this rate."

Three men died in the raid—two marines of the fighter squadron and a sailor at what remained of the naval air station. They were buried, and the familiar cleanup-restore-repair work went on for the rest of the day. Later, when the men tried to piece together the story of that day, it was lost amidst the confused memories of so many other days just like it. They would strain to remember whether it had been Sunday or Monday or perhaps even Wednesday. The calendar was muddled and time distorted. The only things they knew for sure were that the bombers came over and men died, and the living dragged themselves out of shelters and foxholes and ached for sleep. And whether it was a Sunday or a Monday did not make any difference.

Very early the next morning, Major Putnam was patrolling in his Wildcat southwest of the atoll. He spotted something in the water and dropped down to take a closer look. It was a submarine. He was about to begin a diving attack, but then he hesitated; there was something familiar about the sub's orange markings. He had seen the same markings months ago at Pearl Harbor on Dutch PBY Catalinas bound for the Dutch East Indies. Thinking it was a Dutch sub, Putnam resumed his patrol, but when he landed and reported the sighting, Commander Cunningham was disturbed.

Had it been Dutch, Cunningham pointed out, it would have let Wake know it was in the vicinity; and even if it had not, it wouldn't risk surfacing in daylight.

"From now on," Cunningham said, "all submarines found will be attacked."

Putnam's presence had caused the submarine to dive, and apparently as a result, there was no noon raid that day. Everyone waited and watched, but no bombers came. There was no damage to repair, but the building continued without pause. At Peacock Point, a group of civilians with a bulldozer carved out two deep underground shelters with roofs of coral rock three feet thick. Other work details were busy around the airfield making deeper and safer bunkers.

At the edge of the field, an ominous activity was under way. Major Bayler and six civilians were tearing all the classified books and manuals of the fighter squadron into shreds and burning them in a large gasoline drum. It took them three hours to destroy all the material. Commander Cunningham had destroyed all the remaining code material some days before and had ordered Bayler to do the same. Even though Bayler said it was satisfying to know that the papers would never fall into enemy hands, he considered it melodramatic and unnecessary because Wake would never fall; it would never be allowed to fall. "Wake was an outpost of a mighty nation," he wrote, "and in due time, not too far distant, we would be sent the reinforcements needed to hold the fort."

It looked as though it would be Wake's second day without a raid, and the men began to relax. About 5:30 that afternoon, they spotted a plane in the distance dodging in and out of clouds. Then it was gone. A half-hour later, however, just as darkness was falling, some four-engine flying boats appeared from the east. Reports vary as to how many there were (from four to six), but there was no mistaking the bombs they dropped on Peale or their low-altitude strafing run over all three islands.

On the beach near Peacock Point, Private Michael Olenowski aimed his .50 caliber machine gun at the planes. Bullets ripped into the coral all around him, but still Olenowski stayed at his gun and returned the fire. The planes roared low overhead, and he swiveled the gun around and kept firing. The planes disappeared out over the lagoon beyond his range of fire, and still he kept shooting. A noncom yelled at him to stop firing, but he couldn't. Finally he had to pull his hand off the trigger with his free hand. He said later that he didn't know a man could be so tired.

On the evening of December 15 in Pearl Harbor, the ships of the relief force got under way. The size of the force—*Saratoga,* three cruisers, nine destroyers, *Tangier,* and the oiler *Neches*—was an indication of how badly the Pacific Fleet had been damaged. These few ships, a single squadron of planes, and about 200 marines were all that could be spared to relieve an important island bastion. One of the ships, the *Neches,* was an unfortunate though unavoidable choice. It had a maximum speed of only twelve knots, and that only in a fair wind, its crew said.

Despite the small size of the relief force and the uncertain waters into which it was sailing, the ships' crews, as well as the marines they carried, were excited at the chance to meet the enemy. No one was certain what faced them, but the odds were not encouraging. Japanese submarines lurked throughout Pacific waters. Johnston and Midway Islands had been shelled, and the whereabouts of the fleet that had attacked Pearl Harbor was still unknown. The men of the small, understrength task force fully expected to meet a major Japanese fleet. They were expendable, they thought—doomed, but determined to take as many of the enemy as possible with them. Not a single sailor jumped ship at Pearl Harbor, despite the odds they thought they were facing. No one wanted to miss this chance.

It was twilight when the ships passed out of Pearl. All hands looked at the wreckage of a Japanese bomber tossing in the surf just offshore from Fort Kamehameha. In the channel, they glided softly by the battleship *Nevada,* damaged and beached in front of a field of green sugar cane. Out they sailed, beyond sight of land, the first American fleet to venture west of Hawaii since December 7.

Early the next morning the marines on board the *Tangier* turned out with enthusiasm for dawn General Quarters and began intensive training and preparation for the relief of Wake. They cleaned and oiled their weapons, sharpened bayonets to a razor edge, and studied every available map. The three-inch antiaircraft gun crews, anticipating that they might have to fire against ships or ground targets in the coming battle, designed different sights for their guns and made them in the *Tangier's* machine shop.

The machine gun crews, with the help of sailors, built slings which they could use to hoist their weapons onto barges in full firing position so as to be able to fight their way through the enemy onto the beaches. The five-inch gun crews practiced their work at the ship's five-inch gun, standing in for the naval crew. Lectures were given on the problems of disembarking and unloading equipment at Wake. Plans were formulated for lightering in men and weapons. If the *Tangier* was damaged before the men had disembarked, the captain had orders to run the ship aground. Harried officers tried to plan for every contingency.

Even the mail situation was anticipated. On the premise that fighting would be too heavy to allow the replacement troops time to write letters, several hundred canned message postcards were prepared in the ship's printshop. At the bottom of each card was the optimistic line: "P.S. We have the situation well in hand." Slowly and warily the force moved westward, with tension mounting as each day passed into the next. Every day news reports raced through the ships: "They hit Wake again today." Marines passed the word, and their anger and determination grew as they became more impatient to join their brothers on the beaches.

The bombers came back to Wake on Tuesday, December 16. There were twenty-three of them at 18,000 feet, and they were spotted early by two Wildcat pilots, Lieutenants Kinney and Kliewer. They darted in and out of the formation but had no luck and pulled away when the bombers reached the atoll at 1:15. The three-inch guns opened up immediately, and puffs of smoke dotted the V-formations. One plane fell into the sea, and four others limped away trailing smoke. There was no damage on the ground; most of the bombs fell harmlessly into the lagoon.

At 6:00 that evening, a lone flying boat appeared over the island, darting out of low rain clouds. It dropped four bombs around Battery D on Peale and strafed the position heavily. It was Wake's tenth air raid, and the ninth day of the war.

But the day was not yet over. A heavy drizzle was falling when, at 2:00 A.M., lookouts on Wilkes Island reported ships not far offshore. Major Devereux was awakened, and he climbed atop his command post to scan the sea. He saw nothing, but other posts reported in with the same message: twelve ships close in. It looked like what they had been expecting—a night landing.

Every man was alerted, every weapon manned. At the airfield, the marines of VMF-211 assembled and formed up as a ground force. They were told to stand by until it was known which beach the Japanese were landing on. Armed with rifles and pistols, they stood ready to repel an invasion—all twenty of them.

The minutes passed. Fingers stretched taut on triggers, eyes narrowed to peer through the rain and darkness, but nothing happened. The ships, if there were any, sailed away. The men waited an hour for their return; then Devereux ordered half of them to remain on watch while the rest slept by their guns. They stayed that way until dawn, but the mystery ships were gone.*

And so it continued, each day an increasingly vague and confused blur. There were twenty-seven planes at 1:17 one day and eight flying boats at dusk, twenty-seven bombers at 10:50 on another day, and two more enemy planes shot down. A diesel oil tank was set ablaze on Wilkes, what was left of the tents in Camp 1 destroyed, the evaporator needed for water purification damaged. Camp 1 was hit again and turned into a barren landscape of debris and craters. What little remained of the naval air station and the Pan American compound was churned over again by more bombs. Machine gun bullets raked over the debris and sought out men's flesh. And then camouflage was restored, more shelters were dug, and the lookouts scanned the sky and the sea. Men fell asleep on their feet and stumbled into craters in the darkness and listened for the sound of engines above the surf and were grateful for an hour of sleep. And

* The appearance of the ships remains a mystery to this day. Postwar examination of Japanese records found no evidence of ships off Wake that night, and no American ships were that close.

each day passed like the day before.

The air force grew and diminished. One day there were four planes miraculously compounded out of parts and pieces and ingenuity. A few hours later, one would crash on takeoff for reasons unknown and join the scrap heap or come alive again as a hybrid, a bastard airplane of unknown and dubious heritage. Lieutenant Kinney, Sergeant Hamilton, Aviation Machinist's Mate Hesson, and some civilian volunteers worked through the nights and days, falling asleep for a half-hour under a wing, then climbing back on a ladder to work on a worn-out engine.

Major Putnam described it as "a truly remarkable and almost magical job. With almost no tools and a complete lack of normal equipment, they performed all types of repair and replacement work. They changed engines and propellers from one airplane to another, and even completely built up new engines and propellers from scrap parts salvaged from wrecks. They replaced minor parts and assemblies, and repaired damage to fuselages and wings and landing gear; all of this in spite of the fact that they were working with new types with which they had had no previous experience and were without instruction manuals of any kind. In the opinion of the squadron commander their performance was the outstanding event of the whole campaign."

Life continued, and certain routines came to be accepted as normal. Dan Teters's chuck wagon catering service rolled around to major points on the atoll at dawn and dusk to bring hot food. If a man got hungry in between, he could walk into the woods and find food at one of the caches stored there. Hardtack and jam were always available.

In the hospitals, the wounded and the sick could only stare in the darkness at the domed concrete ceiling whenever the bombers came over. The doors would be quickly shut; then the staff would place tongue depressors in the patients' mouths and tell them to clench down hard with their teeth when the bombs fell. The lights would be turned out, and the patients would lie there feeling the ground shake all around them.

When a raid was particularly heavy, patients were moved to the lower level by the light of dim emergency lamps. Sometimes after a raid there was no time to move them back up before new wounded were brought in. The operating table was on the lower level—rough plank boards with crude equipment—but in the hands of the two surgeons, lives were saved under those primitive conditions. The navy doctor, Lieutenant Kahn, was one of the hardest-working men on the entire atoll. He hardly ever went outdoors, and his skin was sallow and pasty. His eyes were dark circles from lack of sleep, his face bearded from lack of time to shave. He always wore hospital pajamas. His counterpart in the civilian hospital, Dr. Shank, worked equally hard under equally primitive conditions. He would die on Wake Island—but not for two more years.

Then there was Sergeant Raymon Gragg, former soldier and wrestler and an excellent marine, but one who had some exasperating moments. Sergeant Gragg was very concerned about his feet, and he constantly harangued his men about taking care of theirs. Since there were few chances to bathe on Wake, foot powder became a high-priority item to Gragg. One day he heard that one of the contractor's supply dumps had some foot powder. That night he groped around the area in the darkness until he found the familiar shape of a foot powder can. He took a bath in the lagoon and liberally sprinkled his feet and the insides of his shoes with the powder. Then he went back to his position to sleep, fully dressed (as everyone slept).

Barely had he fallen asleep when he suddenly jumped up. Rats were climbing all over him. He beat them away, but they kept returning. They were particularly attracted to his shoes and chewed on the leather as though they were trying to get inside. It took Sergeant Gragg a long time to figure out what had happened—the can had contained powdered cheese!

Sergeant Gragg was gun captain of one of the three-inch antiaircraft guns, a job that required him to wear earphones. During one raid, he kept his gun firing until the last possible second, then ordered his men to the shelter as bombs started to fall all around. When his men were safe, Gragg ran for the dugout thirty feet away but forgot to remove his earphones. He was almost there—just ten feet from the shelter's entrance—when the twenty-foot cord caught up with him and violently yanked him backwards, flat on his back. The bombs were too close for him to get up. All he could do was roll over and put his arms over his head. He wasn't injured in the raid, but it took him awhile to get over the grinning faces of his men when they came out of the dugout. One young marine smiled at him and asked, "Did the sergeant hurt himself?"

Private First Class Verne L. Wallace was not happy being in the marines. A year before he had had a nice job in a movie theater in Philadelphia. A friend taunted him into coming with him to the marine recruiting office. Wallace was short and skinny, and his friend bet him that the marines wouldn't want him. Well, they did want him, but they turned down his friend. "Every time I'm under fire," he said to a buddy, "I keep thinking, 'What the hell am I doing here?' I ought to be in Philadelphia."

Corporal Bernard E. Richardson wanted to be a writer. No matter how exhausted he was, he wrote at least a few pages each day, and by the time the war started, he had completed a 150,000-word manuscript. He was sent to Wilkes when the war broke out, and he fretted every day over the safety of his novel. Finally, during the second week of the war, he had a chance to return to Wake. He ran to his tent, but it was gone—all the tents were gone. He searched through the debris but never found even a single page of his manuscript. Later, in a prison camp, he collected every scrap of paper he could find and began to rewrite his story. He had finished about 40,000 words when the Japanese discovered it and destroyed it. "I guess I better stick to short stories till I get home," he said to a friend.

The Deacon was an unusual marine. A former prizefighter, Sergeant Orville M. Cain was a very religious man. He always carried a Bible with him and was constantly reading it or quoting from it. He never used profanity and would not permit beer drinking or card playing in his tent, and he was big and tough enough not to be challenged by his tentmates. If they wanted to play poker or pitch pennies, they went outside. Sergeant Cain never expressed any hatred of the Japanese, unlike the rest of the men on Wake. As a gun captain he shot at them and killed them, but when an enemy plane exploded in the air or fell into the sea, he would say, "God bless you, brother!" and switch his sights to the next target.

Messages kept coming in from the brass at Pearl Harbor, advice from comfortable offices 2,000 miles away on how to fight in the front line. One that was particularly galling to Major Devereux concerned window glass. The message said that if there was not enough glass for the barracks windows, seismographic paper could be used instead. It was true that there wasn't enough glass to replace the shattered windows, but it made no difference because the barracks had all been blown apart anyway.

Devereux wrote to Colonel Bone at Pearl Harbor to complain about such idiotic instructions. "The brass hats who thought up these silly messages had better get down to earth."

Commander Cunningham was irate about a message which urged the Wake defenders to continue dredging the Wilkes channel and asked when it would be completed. Cunningham was so angry that he waited a full day before replying. Prefacing his communique with a report of the latest bombing attacks, he went on to summarize the situation. At least half of the trucks and construction equipment had been destroyed, most of the diesel fuel and commercial explosives were gone, and the garage, machine shops, and the warehouse full of building supplies had been leveled.

His fury mounted as he wrote out the message.

"To date, have been concerned only with defense of island and preservation of life. Reports submitted have been from that viewpoint. Regard to completion of channel following conditions prevail. No work can be carried on at night due necessity for lights. Daylight hours for work limited to maximum of six due heavy raids which come without warning. Have no radar. Men working noisy equipment cannot be warned in time. Equipment greatly reduced with no repair facilities. Would require immediate replenishment diesel oil and dynamite. Morale civilian workmen in general very low. Under present conditions no date completion can be predicted."

He read it over and then added another sentence.

"To be understood that relief from raids would improve outlook."

He received no more messages about the progress of construction.

One day stood out clear and sharp from all the others in the period of attrition that marked the second phase in the battle for Wake. December 20 was the second Saturday of the war, and it began dark and overcast with a drenching rain. It was a gloomy morning, and visibility was poor—and the marines could not have been happier about it. They hoped the overcast would last all day, because it might keep the enemy away.

At 7:00, the most exciting message ever received on Wake came through from Midway. A navy PBY patrol plane was on its way, and as word of it raced around the island, every man asked the same question: what is it bringing—supplies, reinforcements? That had been on everyone's mind for days.

A few days before that, Captain Elrod had stopped at the command post to talk to Devereux.

"Why the hell doesn't somebody come out and help us fight?" Elrod asked, but Devereux had no answer.

Now, Major Devereux thought, maybe they would get an answer.

The radioman picked up signals from the PBY as the pilot sent out weather reports in plain English every hour.

"The damn fool must think he's on a picnic," one of the Wake fliers said. "Why doesn't he just invite the Japs to come get him?"

All through the day they waited, and the odds that the ship would be shot down before it reached them got higher, but at 3:30 it glided in and landed gently in the lagoon.

A few tired, dirty, and disheveled marines were standing at what was left of the dock as the plane taxied up. They watched a very young ensign in a clean, starched uniform climb out. He walked up to them and asked, "Where's the Wake Island Hotel?"

The marines stared at him in disbelief, at first unable to reply. When the pilot was about to ask again, a private gestured to a pile of rubble and answered, "Sir, that's it."

Commander Cunningham soon appeared in the civilian pickup truck that he used for a staff car. The pilot and copilot, Ensigns James J. Murphy and H. P. Ady, were wide-eyed with surprise as Cunningham drove them to his command post. It was obvious they had not known how heavily Wake had been bombed.

Along with official mail for Cunningham and Devereux, the plane brought the news everyone had hoped for—reinforcements were on the way and would arrive on the twenty-fourth. The official dispatch spelled out exactly what was coming on the *Tangier* as well as the squadron of planes on the *Saratoga* that would be Wake's new air force. It was like Christmas five days early. They would survive after all. With new planes and men and materiel they could hold Wake.

The orders also indicated that all but 350 of the most essential construction workers would be taken off the island by the ships of the relief force, and Dan Teters immediately made up a roster of those who would stay. Major Bayler, whose orders called for him to proceed to Midway on the earliest transportation, was alerted to leave on the PBY early the next morning. And all over the island that afternoon and evening men wrote letters. It was the first chance in a long time to get mail out, and they wrote to wives, sweethearts, and mothers assuring them that all was well on Wake.

Cunningham, Devereux, and Putnam wrote official reports on the status of their commands. Cunningham tried once more to convey to his superiors just how much damage had been suffered and to praise his command.

"Our escape from more serious damage may be attributed to the effectiveness of AA fire and the heroic actions of the fighter pilots who have never failed to push home attacks against heavy fire. The performance of these pilots is deserving of all praise. They have attacked air and surface targets alike with equal abandon."

When he finished his official correspondence, Cunningham's thoughts turned to his wife and daughter, living in Annapolis, Maryland. He wrote them an optimistic, cheery letter which reflected his newly revived hope for the future, now that Wake was being reinforced.

"Dear Wife and Kid—We are having a jolly time here and everything is in good shape. I am well and propose to stay that way. Hope you are both in the pink and having a good holiday season. Trust you haven't worried about me, for you know I always land on my feet. . . .

"The situation is good and is getting better. Before

long you won't hear of a Japanese east of Tokyo. The climate is good, the food isn't bad, and I only have to wash my face once a day. Baths even scarcer, though we work in a swim now and then.

"You know I am waiting only for the time of our joining. Circumstances may delay it a little longer, but it will surely come."

He added more personal words to his wife, sealed the envelope, and smiled at the suddenly improved prospects and how happy his wife would be when the news about Wake's relief was known.

Major Devereux finished all his official correspondence that night in his command post and started a letter to his wife and son. "There was much I wanted to tell them, deeply personal things, and some things that seemed important to me I wanted to tell my son in case I didn't come through."

Slowly he began to write—a few words, one line, then two—then he stopped. He stared for a long time at the words, then shook his head. He could not bring himself to say what he wanted to. He tore up the page and went back to work.

The busiest man of all that afternoon and night was Major Bayler. Everyone knew he was leaving and that his assignment on Midway was temporary, after which he would go back to Pearl. Many men came to him asking if he would send telegrams to their families when he got back to Honolulu. He decided he'd have to restrict it to the wounded, and that night he made the rounds from cot to cot and wrote down a few words from each man. He promised to send the messages as soon as he could.

"To Mrs. J. R. Lanning, 320 D Street, National City, California: 'OK, Chick.'

"To Mrs. Neil Gooding, of Gooding, Idaho: 'OK from Boyce.'

"To V. F. Webb, 110 Military Street, Oxford, North

Carolina: 'OK, everything fine, from Gorham.'

"To Mrs. Luther Williams, of Stonewall, Mississippi: 'Solon is OK. Tough fight—but OK.' "

There were others—it was a long list—but the telegrams were never sent. By the time Bayler reached Honolulu, it was too late.

There was one other person who planned to be a passenger on the PBY. The Bureau of the Budget official, Mr. Hevenor, had been dodging bombs and bullets for twelve days and was anxious to leave the atoll, reinforcements or no. It was all arranged; the pilot said there was plenty of room for another passenger, but then a hitch developed. There was only one extra parachute and life jacket aboard, and they were given to Major Bayler, who was on official assignment. A crestfallen Mr. Hevenor was told that he could not go after all because navy regulations did not allow passengers on board without a parachute or life jacket. It would not be safe, he was told.

A little before 7:00 the next morning, Ensign Murphy turned over his engines and made ready for the long flight back to Midway. On the dock, Major Bayler said his good-byes to a group of officers and men who had come to see him off. Time was short. They laughed and grinned and shook hands. "I'll be seeing you," they all said, and then Bayler climbed into the plane. He was sorry to be leaving Wake. There were good friends there—some from other posts and times and some newly met—and they had all shared something important.

"I looked at our flag," Bayler wrote, "still snapping in the breeze at the top of the pole where it had been hoisted on December 8. I looked at the cheerful, grinning faces and the confident bearing of the youngsters on the dock. As I waved a last good-by and took my seat in the plane, my smile was as cheerful as theirs.

"I *knew* all would go well with Wake Island."

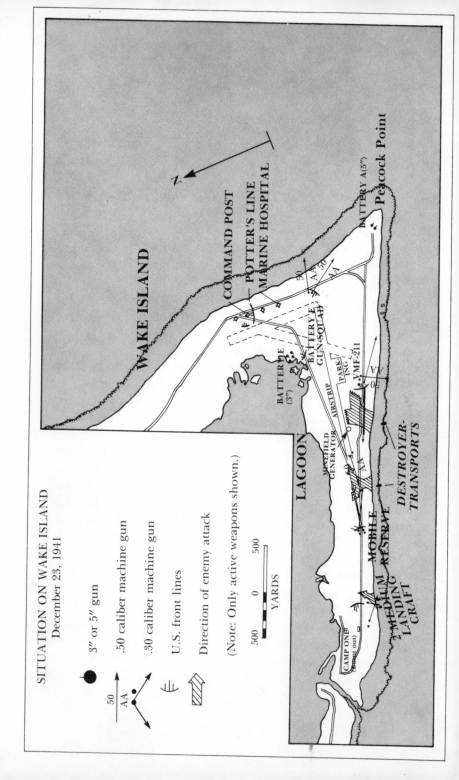

SITUATION ON WAKE ISLAND
December 23, 1941

3" or 5" gun

50   .50 caliber machine gun
AA

.30 caliber machine gun

U.S. front lines

Direction of enemy attack

(Note: Only active weapons shown.)

YARDS
500   0   500

WAKE ISLAND

LAGOON

CAMP ONE
(being out)

MOBILE
RESERVE
2 MEDIUM
LANDING
CRAFT

DESTROYER-
TRANSPORTS

AIRFIELD
GENERATOR

AIRSTRIP

PARK-
ING

VMF-211

BATTERY E
GUN-SQUAD

BATTERY E
(3")

COMMAND POST

POTTER'S LINE

MARINE HOSPITAL

AA

50

AA

AA

AA

BATTERY A (5")

Peacock Point

N

7

"There Are Japanese in The Bushes"

Less than two hours after the PBY took off, the war on Wake took a new and ominous turn, one that would spell defeat in a day or two unless the reinforcements arrived first. The sky was heavily overcast, so there was no warning of the attack. Only one Wildcat was in flying condition that morning, but because of the weather it had not been sent up.

At 8:50 they came out of the clouds—twenty-nine dive bombers and eighteen fighters. What made their appearance so alarming was not their number, but the fact that they were navy planes. That meant only one thing: a carrier was out there somewhere over the horizon, and it would not be alone. An invasion force would be with it.

The planes swept in so low and fast that the three-inch guns did not have time to aim and fire. Major Putnam was in the vicinity of Camp 2 when the attack began, and he jumped in his truck and started back to the airfield. The dive bombers pounced on him, and he slammed on the brakes and dove into a ditch with machine gun bullets kicking up sand all around him. Twice he had to bail out of the truck when planes attacked him, but he made it to the field and climbed into the cockpit of the lone serviceable plane. The Japanese had finished their attack by the time he roared down the runway, but he raced after them anyway. The plane, unfortunately, wasn't up to it, and he had to turn around and limp back to the field before he had a chance to catch up with them.

The planes did little damage, but the knowledge that a carrier was close by was damaging enough. The optimism of the previous night faded and was replaced by a cautious hope that the relief force might still reach them in time. It was going to be a race between the two fleets. Commander Cunningham dispatched word of the carrier to Pearl and marked it "Urgent."

As the carrier-based planes were swooping over Wake, the amphibious assault force under the command of Admiral Kajioka sailed out of the harbor at Roi-Namur and headed north to link up with Admiral Abe's carrier force.

Three hours later, at 12:20, thirty-three twin-engine bombers appeared from the east over Wake in two formations at 18,000 feet. One group headed for Camp 2, and the other concentrated on Peale Island. In the director pit of Battery D, a legendary Marine Corps figure calmly supervised the fire of his ack-ack guns. Platoon Sergeant Johnalson E. "Big" Wright was said to be the fattest man in the corps. He could drink a keg of beer in record time, and the scuttlebutt was that he weighed 320 pounds.

Yet there was no better marine around. Calm and professional, he knew his job and did it well. Big Wright was indeed the stuff of legends. He had a lucky dollar—a silver dollar—that he played with in his huge hand whenever things got rough. The bombs would come closer and closer, and his crew would look at him, waiting for the word to take cover, but he'd say nothing.

He would wait until the last possible moment.

"OK. Hit the hole," he'd shout.

He'd watch his men run for the shelter, and slowly he would squat down in the corner of his pit and sit there while the bombs fell.

In the middle of a raid, he'd yell, "Hey Godwin!"

Platoon Sergeant William Godwin would call back from his dugout, "Yo!"

"Don't you worry, Godwin! I'm squeezing my lucky dollar for you!"

Soon the raid would be over, and the men would crawl out of their shelter and look at Big Wright as he stood up and brushed himself off.

"Lucky dollar worked again," somebody would say.

"It always works," Wright would answer.

No one knew where Sergeant Wright got his lucky dollar or how it came to be lucky. Other old-timers who had served with Wright before said he had it back in '31 in the fighting in Nicaragua. But it really didn't make any difference where it came from, not to the men of Battery D. Whenever anyone would scoff at the idea of a good-luck piece, one of his men always answered, "We're still alive, aren't we?"

It impressed one young marine so much—the sight of Big Wright sitting out in the open with bombs bursting all around him—that he wanted a good-luck piece of his own. Private First Class Bernard A. Dodge asked everyone he could find, but nobody had a silver dollar. He settled for a fifty-cent piece. When the bombs fell, Dodge would hunch down in the generator pit and squeeze his lucky half-dollar.

"Maybe it was crazy," Devereux wrote, "but it was something to hang onto, and there are times when a man needs that."

The Japanese bombers plastered Peale Island on the twenty-first. Big Wright kept his men at the guns long enough to fire thirty-five rounds, long enough to hit one of the planes before he sent them to the shelters.

"Hey Godwin!" his voice boomed out over the explosions. "Don't you worry, Godwin! I'm squeezing my lucky dollar for you!"

Suddenly the air filled with sand and smoke and flying jagged steel splinters. The earth heaved, and the sound of the explosion muted the roar of the surf and the drone of engines. The blast knocked men flat against the ground. Its force tore the clothes off Sergeant Steve Fortuna. Blinded for a moment, gasping and choking, Fortuna staggered on his hands and knees, calling out to his buddy, Big Wright. There was no answer. They found the lucky dollar still clutched tightly in his dead fingers.

Three men were wounded in the raid and were taken to the hospital. A group of Sergeant Wright's men dug a grave near the battery and placed him gently in it. When they finished, Private First Class Dodge walked down to the edge of the island and looked out over the lagoon, holding his half-dollar in his hand. Then he drew his arm back as far as he could and threw the coin into the water.

The bomb that killed Big Wright seriously weakened the antiaircraft defense of the whole atoll, for it totally destroyed the directional firing equipment of Battery D. Battery F on Wilkes had never had any fire-control apparatus, so now the only director for all of the ack-ack guns was at Battery E on Wake Island near the airstrip. But that battery had no height finder, which Battery D did have. Thus there was only enough fire-control equipment for one battery of guns. Some units would have to be moved.

With a crew of 125 civilians, some of the equipment and one gun from Battery D on Peale were moved to Battery E on Wake. This became the only fully manned, fully equipped antiaircraft battery. The remaining guns on Peale were split up, two moved to a point where they could serve as beach defense weapons, and the third remaining in the old position along with dummy guns to fool the Japanese into thinking the battery was in full operation.

Meanwhile, Major Devereux was trying to strengthen his beach defenses at those points where enemy troops would most likely try to land—the southern beaches of Wake and Wilkes. Here the coral reef was considerably closer to the shore than at any other place along the coastline. Even trying to defend this one stretch of coastline was difficult with the small number of men available.

The marines of the defense battalion worked well into the night again, digging, camouflaging, and sandbagging. At dusk Major Devereux walked along the beach talking to the men, making sure everything was as tight as it could be.

"I noticed a strange thing," Devereux wrote. "It was an unspoken thing, intangible, but it was as real as the sand or the guns or the graves. My men were average marines, and they had bitched and griped among themselves like any soldiers. Now their nerves and bodies had been sapped by two almost sleepless weeks. Now the chips were down for the last roll of the dice, and they knew it, and they knew the odds were all against us, but now they were not grumbling. There seemed to grow a sort of stubborn pride that was more than just the word 'morale.' "

Devereux told of a gun captain, Corporal Hershel L. "Moss" Miller, who drove his crew and his gun faster each time the enemy planes came over, faster than anybody had ever seen a three-inch gun fire. After the planes left earlier that day, Miller slumped down wearily, his eyes glazed.

"If they want this island," he said, "they gotta pay for it."

"That," said Devereux, "was how it was on Wake as our time ran out."

Men worked all through the night preparing revetments for the new squadron of planes that was somewhere out there on the decks of the *Saratoga*. In their lightproof hangar, Kinney and Hamilton somehow constructed another plane so that in the morning there would be two for the dawn patrol. Lieutenant Kinney could hardly stand up, so weak was he from diarrhea, but he refused to go to the hospital.

In the hours before dawn, men dropped off for a bit of sleep though there was a full list of projects still to work on. They were projects that would not be finished.

While the defenders of Wake worked through the night of December 21–22, the relief force was sailing westward, though still at a speed of only twelve knots because of the slow oiler. This was half the speed the rest of the ships could make. At 10:00 that night, the navigator aboard Admiral Fletcher's flagship, the *Astoria,* plotted their position; they were 627 miles from Wake.

Admiral Fletcher was in constant touch with what was happening on Wake. Cunningham's reports to Pearl Harbor were immediately relayed to the task force, so Fletcher knew that Wake was now being attacked by carrier planes. The admiral was more concerned, however, about the fuel supplies of his eight destroyers, which were sufficient to take them to Wake but not adequate, in his view, should they be forced to maneuver in the event of a battle at sea.*

* This point is disputed by naval historian Admiral Samuel Eliot Morison in his book, *The Rising Sun in the Pacific.* He argues that there was no danger of the destroyers running out of fuel. Morison and others contend that Fletcher should have refueled his destroyers earlier, thus eliminating the need for the slow-moving *Neches.* Fletcher waited, however, until the morning of the twenty-second to refuel.

By the time he decided to refuel on the morning of the twenty-second, the weather had deteriorated, further hampering the always ticklish job of refueling at sea. The wind shifted, forcing a change of direction of some of the ships so that a portion of the force was actually sailing away from Wake. It took all day to fuel four of the destroyers, and by the time they could again set course for Wake, it was dusk. The ships were not much closer to Wake than they had been at 8:00 that morning, and there were four more destroyers to refuel.

On Wake, Second Lieutenant Carl Davidson took off alone for the noon patrol on the twenty-second. The other plane would not start, and it took an hour for the exhausted Kinney and Hamilton to get it running. Captain Freuler pointed the plane down the runway, and it wheezed and coughed as it took off. Both planes, like their pilots, were worn out.

Lieutenant Davidson was cruising north of Wake at 12,000 feet when he saw a large force of carrier planes heading for the atoll. They were in two formations— thirty-three dive bombers at 18,000 feet and six of the new Zero fighters at 12,000 feet. He radioed his find to Freuler, who was just south of Wake. Freuler sped north as fast as his patched-up plane would go and attacked the six fighters while Davidson went after the bombers.

The Zeroes broke formation as Freuler dove into them, and one enemy plane caught fire and fell toward the sea. The planes were twisting and turning all over the sky as Freuler came in for another attack. He lined up his sights on a Zero and felt his plane buck as the four .50 caliber machine guns went into action. The Zero began to wobble as his bullets tore into it.

Freuler broke off his attack at the last possible second, barely avoiding a collision with the plane. Just as he passed over the stricken Zero no more than fifty feet away, it exploded in a giant ball of flame. Steel fragments and fire enveloped Freuler's ship, scorching its aluminum skin, and the blast threw him out of control. Furiously he fought to bring the ship back under control, but it reacted sluggishly, and the manifold pressure began to drop fast.

Suddenly a Zero was on his tail, and he saw holes appear in his wings. Desperately he tried to maneuver, but the Wildcat would not respond. For a second he glanced up and saw Lieutenant Davidson attacking one of the bombers; a Zero hung on his tail too. A sharp hammerblow of pain hit Freuler in the back, then another in the shoulder. The Japanese fighter was still behind him turning his plane into a sieve, and he could not maneuver out of the line of fire.

There was only one thing to do. Freuler put his ship into a steep screaming dive, praying that the bullet-riddled wings would hold on and that enough control surface was intact to pull out. The horizon spun, and he headed the bucking, vibrating plane straight toward the water. The altimeter needle swung wildly as the airspeed built up. He glanced behind him and saw that the Zero was gone, apparently believing he was finished.

With all his strength, he pulled back on the control stick with both hands, but still the plane plummeted downward. Bracing his boots against the floorboards, he pulled even harder until gradually the ship began to level off close to the water. Freuler headed for the airstrip, nursing the sputtering engine every mile of the way.

The engine nearly quit when he came in over the edge of the field. The landing gear was up, but he didn't have the strength to crank it down. The gleaming white strip of coral rose toward him fast, and he tried to level the ship as he braced himself for a crash landing. The plane bounced and scraped on the crushed coral and finally came to a bone-jarring stop. Freuler managed to pull himself out of the cockpit and take one last look at the plane before he was taken off to the hospital. Sadly he shook his head—there would be no reclaiming it.

Minutes later the Japanese planes raked the islands, bombing and strafing. They concentrated on the three-inch batteries but caused no casualties.

Anxious pilots and ground crew looked out to sea all afternoon hoping to see Lieutenant Davidson swoop down for a landing, but he never returned. That was the end of the air battle for Wake Island; VMF-211 ceased to exist as a fighter squadron. There weren't enough parts left to even try to build another plane.

Major Putnam assembled his men and marched to Devereux's command post.

"We're reporting as infantry," he said.

Lieutenant Kinney wanted to come with them. He argued and pleaded, but Putnam was firm; Kinney had to report to the hospital. Dr. Kahn examined him and put him right to bed. On his chart he wrote, "severe diarrhea and complete physical exhaustion."

Devereux worked all afternoon positioning his men and their weapons to repel the invasion everyone knew was coming. On Peale, Wilkes, and Wake, still more foxholes were dug and three-inch guns depressed so they could fire against landing craft. Their crews were instructed to fall back from the beach and deploy as infantry when they could no longer fire their guns.

At dusk Devereux walked along the south beach of Wake again, looking from the sea to his defenses and back, wondering whose ships would appear first over the horizon—Japanese or American. Tomorrow would be the twenty-third of December. The men on Wake had to hold one more day, and then the relief force would arrive. Just one more day, and the day after that, Devereux remembered, was Christmas.

At that moment, Wake was almost completely surrounded by Japanese ships. Admiral Kajioka's invasion
fleet of nine ships was thirty miles to the south. Two
hundred miles north the two carriers and their supporting ships were cruising back and forth, ready to
launch their planes again at the first light of dawn. And
to the east, one hundred fifty miles away, a screening
force of four heavy cruisers, two light cruisers, and two
destroyers was on the lookout for any American ships
that might try to interfere with the landing.

Five hundred miles east of Wake, Task Force 14 was
still sailing at twelve knots. It had been one of the most
frustrating days in Admiral Fletcher's long career. In the
rough seas, towlines had parted and seven fuel lines had
broken, and there were still four more destroyers to refuel. In addition, he had received countermanding and
contradictory orders during the day from Pearl.

Fletcher had the impression that his superiors could
not make up their minds about what they wanted to do,
and he was right. Admiral Kimmel, who had planned
the entire relief operation, no longer commanded the
Pacific Fleet. Ten days after the attack on Pearl Harbor,
he was relieved from active service. Admiral Chester A.
Nimitz was appointed to replace him as CincPac. But
Nimitz was in Washington and wouldn't reach Honolulu
until Christmas day, so someone had to fill in as acting
commander of the fleet.

That assignment was given to Vice Admiral William S.
Pye. An acting commanding officer is in a difficult and
unenviable position. He knows he will be relieved
shortly; there is no time to formulate his own approach
or to gather his own staff. Usually the best he can do is
maintain the status quo until the new commanding
officer arrives to take over.

Pye was a well-respected officer with a good reputation as a strategist, but he was also known to be cautious and conservative. While able to anticipate steps the enemy might take, he was inclined to hold off acting until he knew what was actually happening. His major concern was, understandably, the safety of what remained of the Pacific Fleet. His usual caution was intensified by the example of what had happened to Kimmel. Neither the navy nor the country could afford another naval disaster, and Pye, like anyone else in that position, did not want to be responsible for one.

Where was the Japanese fleet that had attacked Pearl Harbor? No one knew. Many people suspected that at least a portion of it was somewhere between Hawaii and Wake Island, perhaps regrouping for a larger attack on Pearl or an invasion of Hawaii itself. The Pacific Fleet—as much of it as had survived—had to be maintained at all costs so as to be able to defend Hawaii. That was the prime consideration, Pye affirmed in a dispatch to Washington.

Admiral Stark's reply was not encouraging for the defenders of Wake. Wake Island, Stark cabled, had become a liability, and he left it to Pye's judgment whether the garrison there should be evacuated rather than reinforced. Thus Washington put the decision squarely in Pye's hands. On December 21 (December 22 on Wake), Pye and Kimmel's staff agonized over the proper course of action. Ensign Murphy, the PBY pilot, now back in Honolulu after his flight from Wake to Midway, was questioned about the situation on Wake. "Grim, grim, grim," was his reply. Colonel O. T. Pfeiffer and other marine officers there pleaded with Pye, with tears in their eyes, that the expedition be allowed to continue to Wake.

Over the course of that day, Pye and the staff changed their minds several times. First Pye ordered the *Saratoga* to steam at full speed to within 200 miles of Wake and launch her planes to attack the Japanese ships. Before that order could be carried out, it was countermanded.

The next plan wired to Admiral Fletcher ordered him to send the *Tangier* by itself ahead of the task force to evacuate all personnel from Wake. Shortly after its receipt, that order was rescinded. When Pye received word from Wake that it was being attacked by carrier planes, a new and dangerous ingredient was added to the unknown waters ahead of Task Force 14. The *Saratoga* was too valuable a target to risk. And so, as dusk fell over Wake Island, no firm decision had yet been reached at Pearl.

Meanwhile, Admiral Kajioka's amphibious assault force closed to within ten miles of the roaring surf along Wake's south shore. The race was over—the Japanese had won.

There was no moon on the night of December 22, and the lookouts on Wake could see nothing in the blackness. The surf seemed to be pounding more heavily than usual, and the wind was strong as gusty rain squalls blew over the atoll.

Shortly after 10:00, lookouts reported "a hell of a lot of lights" to the northwest. Devereux climbed up on top of his command post and saw a series of brilliant and irregular flashes. Lights at night were nothing new—for the last several nights, lookouts had reported signal flashes out to sea—but these lights were different. There were many more of them, and they were so intense that they appeared to be the firing of naval guns.

Many marines thought it was a naval battle, and that meant only one thing to them—the relief force had arrived a day early and was attacking the enemy ships. Or was it the other way around? Maybe the Japanese were attacking the relief force. The argument raged for awhile, but then the flashes lessened and finally stopped altogether.*

Devereux went back inside and stretched out on a cot. He had barely closed his eyes when Corporal Brown shouted that Japanese troops were reported to be landing on Toki Point.

Devereux jumped up and looked at his watch; it was a little before 1:00 A.M. All over the atoll, marines heard the report from Toki Point on the open telephone line. Without waiting for orders, they scrambled about in the dark to man their battle stations.

Toki Point on Peale Island was precisely opposite from where Devereux thought the invasion would take place. If the report was true, they were in for trouble—their heaviest defenses were on the other side of the atoll. Devereux called First Lieutenant Woodrow M. Kessler, in command of Battery B at Toki Point. Kessler said he saw lights but no sign of a landing. Some of his lookouts had reported small boats just offshore, and so Kessler was manning his beach defenses.

On hearing of the reported landing, Lieutenant Poindexter, in charge of the mobile reserve of eight marines and four machine guns mounted on a truck, assembled his men at their base in Camp 1 and started down the road for Peale. When Major Devereux got word of it, he sent a man out to the road to flag down the truck.

"Stand by until the situation is clarified," he told Poindexter.

Devereux was still convinced that the landing would come on the south shore, and he decided not to react to what he considered a feint on the Peale side of the atoll.

---

* To this day, no one knows what the flashes of light were. Morison has suggested that Japanese gunners were firing at imaginary planes. Heinl believes that enemy gunners thought they were shelling Wake, but were miles off because of an error in navigation.

Reports were coming in now from every unit. All the gun batteries and machine gun emplacements were manned and ready. Wherever a few men could be spared from the gun crews, they were sent to the beaches, rifles in hand. Patrols of three and four men scouted the long open stretches of beach, looking and listening for the enemy.

Devereux called Kessler again to ask if he saw anything.

"There are plenty of lights out there, but that's all."

"Any boats beached?" Devereux asked.

"Negative."

Certain now that there was no landing at Toki Point, Devereux passed the word and told all unit commanders to exercise extreme alertness.

Offshore, rain squalls and heavy winds tossed the ships of the invasion force as they closed on Wake. The landing barges were lowered into the choppy water and the men of the Special Naval Landing Force clambered down the heaving rope nets into them. The barges banged against the steel hulls of the transports and threatened to capsize as the wind and waves caught them broadside. The rest of the landing force aboard the two destroyer-transports dropped their nets and ropes over the sides as the ships turned hard to starboard, increased speed to twelve knots, and headed for the reefs to ram the beach.

Reports of sightings were coming to Devereux one after another. Barges were seen off Peacock Point and all along the south shore of Wake. Lookouts phoned in "movement offshore," "some kind of craft closing in." By then, there was no doubt in Devereux's mind that his prediction was being borne out—the south shore was the target. Somewhere along its four-and-a-half-mile length, Japanese troops would soon come swarming ashore. There were only 200 marines, sailors, and civilians along the coast available to repel more than 1,000 troops now nearing the reefs. More than half of Devereux's men had to remain at their posts manning the five-inch and three-inch guns. That left only about 85 marines for beach defense on Wake, and no more than 45 of those were riflemen (the rest were machine gun crews).

The Japanese landing craft headed toward the beach close to the western end of Wake at a point between the rubble of Camp 1 and the airfield. The two destroyer-transports steamed at full speed toward the reef farther east at a point level with the airstrip.

Black shapes loomed out of the darkness, but no one fired on either side. On board one of the destroyer-transports, the captain yelled, "Shore ahead!" The troops hit the deck, bracing themselves for the crash. To the west, some troops were already out of their landing craft and racing across the beach.

On Wilkes, a six-foot-three marine with a long red beard and a thick British Guards mustache stood in the three-inch battery, straining to hear over the noise of the surf. Gunner Clarence McKinstry, commander of the battery, thought he heard something and yelled at his crew to be quiet. Now he was sure of it, and he called Captain Wesley Platt, the Wilkes commander.

"Captain, I think I hear a motor turning over."

"Can you see anything?" Platt asked in his South Carolina drawl.

"Not a damn thing, but I'm sure it's there. I can hear it."

"Then fire," Platt ordered.

A stream of tracer bullets ripped into the darkness, giving enough light for the men to see a landing boat heading for the beach. The first shots of Wake's final battle had been fired; it was 2:35 A.M. Lieutenant McAlister, commander of the five-inch battery, saw the landing barge and called Platoon Sergeant Henry A. Bedell.

"Send two men to grenade that boat," McAlister ordered.

"Yes sir."

Bedell grabbed Private First Class William Buehler and told him what they were going to do. They scooped up all the grenades they could carry and raced toward the shore. Japanese soldiers were already pouring out of the landing craft and running across the exposed beach. Bedell and Buehler left the protection of the woods and ran across the open sand toward the enemy, throwing hand grenades as they ran. For a moment they were the only marines in the path of the enemy.

Both men were hit; Bedell was killed and Buehler wounded. He stumbled back across the beach and reported to Lieutenant McAlister.

"Sir, they got Bedell. He's dead."

He didn't tell the lieutenant of his own wound but quietly took his place in line to await the Japanese attack.

The .50 caliber tracers swept the area in front of McAlister's position. Shapes appeared in front of the marines, and the Japanese soldiers yelled as they charged. One marine watched a figure run at him; he leaped up with fixed bayonet, and each man plunged his bayonet into the other. They both fell dead.

Meanwhile, Captain Platt telephoned Devereux to get permission to turn on his searchlight to illuminate the beach area. The blinding light cut a huge swath through the night and focused on a landing barge directly in front of the three-inch battery. The light stayed on less than a minute—it never worked well since it had been damaged in a raid—but it was long enough for Gunner McKinstry to get off several rounds of fire. The major force of Japanese headed for the three-inch position, tossing hand grenades into the gun pits. Deadly hand-to-hand fighting followed as the enemy began to overrun the position.

McKinstry, seeing it was hopeless, removed the firing

locks from the guns and ordered his men east toward Lieutenant McAlister's unit. The enemy was on their heels, but the marines' well-aimed fire stopped them.

At this moment, Wilkes Island was suddenly isolated from the rest of the atoll. The telephone link between Captain Platt and Major Devereux's command post on Wake went dead. Not only did that line stop working, but Platt's communications with McAlister and McKinstry were also cut off. Wilkes was now completely on its own, and Captain Platt was out of touch with his major units. The only line left open was to his .50 caliber machine guns located west of McAlister's position. Private First Class S. K. Ray was on that line.

"Captain, they're all around me."

"Can you keep the gun in action?"

"We can try, sir."

Platt heard a heavy burst of fire, then rifle shots and the sound of men yelling; the position was under attack. There was a moment of silence, then Ray came on the line again.

"We're still here, sir."

Platt decided he had to find out what was going on and where his other units were. He left his command post and cautiously made his way through the darkness to locate the rest of his men and prepare to hold his small island.

On Wake Island, the enemy destroyer-transports ground to a jarring halt on the razor-sharp reef. The troops jumped to their feet and began to make their way over the side into the water. The destroyers were too close for the five-inch guns to fire on them, but there was one gun that could be brought to bear—a three-inch gun located on a rise between the airstrip and the shore near where the destroyer-transports had beached. There was only one problem: the gun had no crew.

Second Lieutenant Robert M. Hanna, in command of

the machine guns set up around the airfield, immediately recognized the importance of the gun. With Corporal Ralph J. Holewinski, he raced toward the position. Three civilians—Bob Bryan, Paul Gay, and Eric Lehtola—seeing what was happening, followed after them.*

Major Devereux ordered the men of VMF-211 to set up a defensive line between the beach and the three-inch gun. As Putnam raced away with his eleven officers and eleven men, a group of twenty-two civilian construction workers started to come with them. Putnam turned and yelled at them.

"If you're captured in combat, your chances are mighty poor. You can't go with us."

The leader of the civilians, John P. Sorenson, stepped up to Putnam, towering over him.

"Major," he said, "do you think you're really big enough to make us stay behind."

"I'd be glad to have you as marines. But take off," Putnam said. "Join the other civilians."

Putnam turned and led his men through the darkness. Behind them, crashing through the undergrowth, Sorenson led his men, each one carrying all the ammunition he could.** Putnam placed the men in a skirmish line along the dunes close to the beach, and they waited.

Hanna and his crew reached the three-inch gun and readied it for firing. The gun had no sights, so the best Hanna could do was point it at the nearest destroyer-transport. He opened the breech and peered down the long barrel until he could see his target.

With his first shot he hit the ship squarely on the

---

* Bryan and Gay were later killed, and Lehtola was wounded.

** Sorenson, along with George Fred Gibbons, Ralph Higdon, Red Jones, David Edgar Lilly, Don K. Miller, Jack McKinley, Herschel Lester Peterson, Clinton L. Stevenson, and Harry Yager, was killed.

bridge, spraying the crew and the landing force with shrapnel. The troops scrambled over the side into water almost over their heads as Hanna hit the ship fourteen more times. The area around the ship was light now from the fires set by Hanna's shells, light enough for the marines on shore to see what was happening.

The machine guns on the beach opened up and swept the water around the burning ship. Many Japanese troops were hit, and some ducked underwater to try to make it to the beach, but there was no safety there either. They were pinned down on the sand, unable to move forward or even to return the fire. Machine gun bullets ripped away the gas masks they carried on their backs and zoomed inches over their heads.

"We could not remain thus for much longer," a Japanese soldier wrote. "It was either death or a charge at the enemy.

"An inch at a time we crept toward the enemy. Twenty yards before the enemy, we prepared to charge. All at once a rain of hand grenades came hurtling down on us.

" 'Charge!' the commander's voice rang out. We jumped to our feet and charged. Huge shadows which shouted something unintelligible were pierced one after another. One large figure appeared before us to blaze away with a machine gun from his hip as they do in American gangster films. Somebody went for him with his bayonet and went down together with his victim."

The Japanese charged violently at the thin line held by Putnam and the civilians. It was hand-to-hand fighting in the darkness—a muzzle blast against a man's chest, a bayonet between the ribs, hands closing around a throat. Slowly the Americans fell back, the line bending around the three-inch gun battery, which was still firing. Hanna shifted his fire to the other destroyer-transport and hit it, though it was not set afire.

Other units on Wake peered into the darkness looking

for shapes to come rushing at them, waiting their turn. In the path of the Japanese force heading toward the western end of the airfield, four marines sat quietly, grouped around a generator. Lieutenant Kliewer and three men had been ordered to hold that point and set off the dynamite buried underneath the landing strip if the enemy captured the field. Wires from the generator led to the charges; it was the only way of setting them off.

A thousand yards west of Kliewer's band, Lieutenant Poindexter's force, now composed of twenty marines and fourteen civilians, waited in a thin defensive line where they had been ordered by Devereux. So far they had seen nothing near their position, but suddenly mortars began to fall near them and firing broke out on their right. Poindexter listened for a moment, then located the shots as coming from the south shore near the water tower, not far from Camp 1.

Poindexter left Sergeant T. Q. Wade in command and, spoiling for a fight, drove off in a truck to check out the firing. The four machine guns he was heading for were manned by sailors, and Poindexter thought they might be shooting at shadows. When he reached the nearest emplacement, however, he saw that they were firing at two landing boats. He watched the tracers ricochet off the steel sides of the boats and knew that hand grenades would be the only effective weapons against them.

He picked three men—Boatswain's Mate First Class James E. Barnes, Mess Sergeant Gerald Carr, and Raymond R. Rutledge, a civilian who had served as an officer in the last war. Each man took six grenades and ran down to the shore. The grenades they threw fell short, and they ran back to the machine guns for a fresh supply.

"Let's try again and get closer this time," Poindexter

yelled as he led them back to the beach. One man, watching him run straight for the barges, said he was either "crazy as a bedbug or the bravest guy alive."

This time they made sure they were close enough to do some damage. They waded into the water as far as the reef and tossed their grenades. At that moment the searchlight from Wilkes came on briefly, long enough for them to see that the barges were empty. The Japanese were behind them somewhere on the island.

Around 3:00 A.M., Devereux realized he was losing communications with more of his units. Wilkes was already out of contact. Lieutenant Barninger at the five-inch battery on Peacock Point reported that he was taking machine gun fire; then he too fell silent. Poindexter called from Camp 1 to say he was being attacked on both flanks, and then he lost contact. Devereux tried to reach Putnam but could not raise him. The situation was breaking down rapidly. Without communications, Devereux was increasingly isolated from the fighting.

He ordered Major Potter, the battalion executive officer, to round up all the men he could find and set up a last ditch defensive position across the main road a hundred yards in front of the command post. Potter's force numbered about thirty, mostly clerks and telephone operators. When they pulled out, Devereux was left with two enlisted men, one at the switchboard and the other on the telephone.

Wake Island desperately needed more men, and the only place they could be drawn from was Peale, but there were a limited number who could be spared. Battery B's five-inchers had to be manned and ready in case ships shelled the island from that side or attempted another landing. Only the crews of Battery D's three-inch ack-ack guns could be sent. Fortunately communications were still open to Peale, and Devereux ordered the battery commander, Captain Bryghte D. Godbold, to send one gun section—nine men—to his command post.

Corporal Leon Graves loaded his men on a truck driven by a civilian, and they raced over the road in the darkness to the command post. Devereux ordered Graves to take his men south and join up with the force around Lieutenant Hanna's three-inch gun. The truck took them part of the way; then they had to go on foot through the thick undergrowth toward Hanna's position. They had not moved very far before they were hit by machine gun fire. The marines dropped to the ground and began to fire back at the flashes. Private Ralph Pickett let out a groan and rolled over; he was dead. They were all pinned down in the woods, unable to advance. Finally Graves gave the order to pull back, and they eventually made their way to Major Potter's line.

The fighting was fierce around Hanna's three-inch gun. Putnam's force was pushed further and further back toward the gun. It was close-order fighting, yard by yard, tree by tree. Major Putnam, lying under a bush, suddenly saw two figures loom over him. He fired his .45 at point-blank range, and they both fell, one so close that his helmet clattered against Putnam's.

More firing broke out. Both American and Japanese voices yelled in fury and screamed in pain. The civilian leader, John Sorenson, jumped up and ran toward a group of Japanese, throwing rocks at them until bullets tore into his body and spun him to the ground.

Captain Elrod leaped to his feet. "Kill the sons of bitches!" he yelled, and sprayed the nearby bushes with his submachine gun.

The enemy fell back, but before long they attacked again. A large Japanese force came crashing through the bushes—too many to be stopped this time. Putnam shouted the order to fall back to the gun emplacement. Five of them made it, and they joined Hanna and the two men still alive at his position. "This is as far as we go," Putnam said.

The Japanese swarmed over their position, and the men crawled under the perforated steel platform of the gun mount for protection. A bullet cut across Putnam's cheek and passed through his neck. He felt no pain but wondered why he was suddenly so sleepy. He passed out, came to and cursed loudly, and then passed out again. The Japanese surrounded them and rushed forward in wave after wave, but each time they were beaten back.

It was still raining as the battle continued, but it was beginning to get light. There seemed to be no order to the fighting anymore. Because of the breakdown in communications, it was out of hand, beyond anyone's control. Isolated groups held out, gained ground in short-lived attacks, then fell back again. There was no single front line; the Japanese were overrunning the island at several places.

One frantic civilian staggered into Devereux's command post. He had been with Poindexter's men but had gotten cut off. He was almost incoherent as he slumped on the floor, gasping for breath.

"They're killing 'em all," he said, and told how the Japanese rushed the machine gun positions west of the airfield and bayoneted the crews. He kept repeating himself: "They're killing 'em all."

It was the first news Devereux had of Poindexter's force since communications had been lost. Was Poindexter holding on down by Camp 1? Or was his force broken up and beaten? Did the enemy have all the western part of Wake? What about Wilkes? Was it still in American hands? What happened to Putnam's group? And Corporal Graves with his nine men? No word had been received from him in over an hour. Did Kliewer's men still control the generator? Devereux was besieged by unanswered questions—and there was no way of finding out the answers.

Poindexter's unit was still intact. In fact, it was larger than when it had started out. As his men were slowly pushed back, others—civilians, sailors, marines—stumbled out of the woods and joined them. He now had a force of seventy men plus ten machine guns, but the Japanese kept pressing him back, charging in waves on three sides. The only targets his men could fire at were rifle flashes and elusive shadows which they couldn't see until they were almost on top of them.

Poindexter's men fought hard, but they had to continue their retreat to keep from being outflanked and surrounded. Finally Poindexter decided he would do "the shoving for a change," and he rounded up every man he had and started to push forward. Slowly and painfully they began to regain lost ground and were able to set up a strong defensive perimeter around Camp 1. There they would stand, he said.

In the command post, Corporal Brown was listening intently to a whispered voice coming in over one of the phones. Whoever it was kept repeating the same phrase.

"There are Japanese in the bushes. . . . There are definitely Japanese in the bushes."

"Who's this?" Brown asked. "Where are you?"

"There are Japanese in the bushes. . . . "

Other men listening in on the network heard the voice too, and one of them broke in.

"For Christ's sake, where are you?"

"There are Japanese in the bushes. . . . "

The voice kept saying the same words over and over, monotonously, like a recording. Brown kept asking him where he was, but apparently he didn't hear—at least he never answered.

"He could only whisper into a telephone," Devereux said, "somewhere in the dark.

"Trying to warn us before they got him. Trying to

warn us before he died. But not remembering we could not tell on the network where he was calling from."

The voice said it again and again. Then there was a burst of noise, and the line fell silent.

"I guess they got him," Brown said quietly.

At 4:30 that morning, alarming news reached Devereux's command post from one of the few positions with which he still had contact. At the eastern end of the airfield, overlooking the road coming north from Peacock Point, there was a .50 caliber machine gun section. Commanded by Corporal Winford J. McAnally, the position was held by seven marines and three civilians, and it looked as though a major Japanese force was getting ready to rush it.

Corporal McAnally was in telephone contact with other machine guns north of Peacock Point, and he relayed information from those positions as well as his own to Devereux. In fact, McAnally's was one of the few positions on Wake or Wilkes that Devereux could communicate with, and the young corporal provided most of Devereux's information on how the battle was going.

The machine gun section was in a vital location; it was the only unit between the Japanese and the hospitals and Major Potter's last-ditch defense line. If the enemy overran McAnally's position, they could effectively seal off the western end of Wake from the rest of the island and from Peale as well.

The Japanese slowly moved northward along the road. McAnally spotted them and opened fire with his own guns, directing the fire of the other machine gun section 400 yards south of his position as well. The enemy troops were caught by surprise and quickly pulled back, but not for long. In a massed charge they tried to overwhelm his section, but he beat them back, and his fire cut a bloody swath through the lines of green-clad troops. They fell back again and then tried to sneak up on the position, crawling through the brush to get close enough to use grenades.

McAnally heard them coming and told his men to hold their fire until they got closer. The men waited, listening as the sounds came nearer. Then McAnally yelled, "Fire!" Every machine gun and rifle exploded into action, raking the ground in front of their position. There was sporadic fire in return, but none of it effective, and the enemy retreated, leaving their wounded screaming in the tangled undergrowth.

They tried again, crawling stealthily forward. Others were sent to outflank the position, to surround the Americans and pour hand grenades on them. Again McAnally heard them coming. He placed his nine men around the perimeter of his section and waited until the last nerve-jarring second, until it seemed as though the enemy was right on top of them. Then he opened fire with everything he had. Like the last time, it was impossible to miss; the enemy was so close to the guns and so tightly packed together. The ground around the emplacement became littered with dead and dying, but not one of McAnally's men had been hit.

And again the enemy advanced, creeping near and being torn apart at almost point-blank range. McAnally began to think the Japanese had an inexhaustible supply of men. Each wave was beaten back, but each time they came a little closer to surrounding him.

He could not hold out for too much longer; he had to have more men and fresh supplies of ammunition. He called Major Devereux at the command post.

"Sir, we got to have some help if we're going to hold this."

Devereux told McAnally there were no reinforcements and gave him permission to withdraw.

McAnally sighed.

"Well, sir," he said, "I reckon we can make out a little longer," and he braced himself for the next attack.

About 1,000 yards west of Corporal McAnally's position, Lieutenant Kliewer and his three men were holding out next to the landing strip. With him were Staff Sergeant J. F. Blandy and Sergeants R. E. Bourquin, Jr. and C. E. Trego. To stand off the enemy they had two submachine guns, three pistols, and two boxes of hand grenades. Miraculously they had survived the night without injury.

Theirs was one of the first positions hit, for they were directly in line with the main thrust of Japanese troops who came ashore from the two destroyer-transports. They had been under continuous siege since shortly after 2:00 A.M. Their communications line had been cut, and they were surrounded by the enemy. The Japanese charged their position with fixed bayonets but were beaten back each time. Between the attacks the men discussed in whispers whether or not they should blow up the field while it was still dark enough for them to have a chance to slip away.

Kliewer vetoed the idea. Their orders were clear: blow up the landing strip if it looks like the Japanese have captured it. Kliewer was determined to hang on until the battles raging all over the atoll were decided one way or the other. If the planes of the relief force flew in the next day, they would need the landing strip.

Gradually the first dim light of the new day appeared. The Japanese were massed all around them, ready to make a charge that the four-man position could not stop. The marines could see the size of the force surrounding them, and they looked at one another with the fatalistic half-smiles of doomed men.

"Here they come," one of them yelled, and a wave of troops began to run toward them. Kliewer and his men fired their weapons and reloaded as fast as they could and threw hand grenades one after the other. Many of the Japanese fell, but the rest came on.

Suddenly the chatter of a .50 caliber machine gun was heard from the extreme western edge of the landing strip. The sandbagged machine gun emplacement had been there all along, unnoticed by the Japanese. Now it was light enough for the machine gunners to see the 150 yards to Kliewer's position, and they opened fire. The enemy was caught out in the open, and the heavy fire cut them down like a giant scythe. The dead tumbled and piled atop one another, and the survivors fled in panic.

When the attack was over, Kliewer noticed scores of Japanese flags all along the shore and clusters of them at many points further inland, too. He decided it was time to blow up the landing strip.

"We'll set her off," he said, "and then retreat to that .50 caliber position behind us."

He pressed the button to turn on the generator, but nothing happened. He pressed again, but it refused to start. The heavy rains of the night had drowned out the motor. They started to work on it, but shortly the Japanese attacked again. Together with the machine gun they beat them back, but the enemy persisted. The Japanese tried crawling to within hand grenade range as well as frontal attacks, but each time they left more dead behind them when they retreated. In between the battles, Kliewer and his men kept working on the motor. He was determined not to give the Japanese a landing strip to use.

On Peale Island, all the men could do was wait. All through the dark hours of the night, they listened to the battle and watched the flashes of rifle fire and the graceful sweeping curves from tracer bullets of the machine guns. Commander Cunningham received periodic reports from Major Devereux, none of which were very encouraging. Much earlier in the night he had sent a message to Pearl Harbor.

"Enemy apparently landing."

Then he remembered the two American submarines somewhere off· Wake. If they were close enough, perhaps they could do some damage to the ships of the landing force.

He sent a message in plain English—time was too crucial to bother with code—directing the subs to attack the Japanese ships. An answer came very quickly, but it was not from the submarines. It was from Admiral Pye, and it ended any hopes Cunningham may have had about getting help of any kind in time.

"No friendly vessels in your vicinity nor will be within the next twenty-four hours."

The submarines had been withdrawn.*

Pye's message ended with "Keep me informed."

In the early dawn, at 5:00, Cunningham sent another message, to keep Admiral Pye informed. As he sat down to write out the dispatch, a line from a book he had read sixteen years before suddenly came to his mind. " 'For three days,' Anatole France wrote in *Revolt of the Angels,* 'the issue was in doubt.' "

The phrase seemed appropriate for the situation on Wake and, Cunningham thought, perhaps hopeful as well. He tore off the page and handed it to the coder.

"Enemy on Island—Issue in Doubt."

But there could be little doubt as Cunningham and the others on Peale Island looked across the lagoon at dawn. The American flag still flew over Camp 1, but there were Japanese flags wherever they looked on both Wake and Wilkes.

---

* One of the submarines, *Tambor,* had been ordered to Pearl on the sixteenth because of mechanical problems. The other sub, *Triton,* was ordered further south on the twenty-first. CincPac wanted no possibility of the sub mistaking the relief force for a Japanese fleet and attacking it.

At 5:30, Devereux phoned Captain Godbold on Peale and ordered him to send the entire crew of Battery D and Peale's few machine gunners to Wake, thus virtually stripping Peale of its defenses. Only the men of the five-inch battery and Cunningham's communications personnel were left. Captain Godbold loaded his thirty officers and men on two trucks and headed across the causeway to Wake; they were the final reserves anywhere on the atoll.

Private First Class Wallace was on the first truck, still feeling that he should be in Philadelphia, that being in the marines was all a mistake. He sat on a bench, crowded against Private First Class Albert Breckenridge.

"I bet we never see the sun rise," Breckenridge said.

The truck stopped, and an officer ordered everyone out. The men looked around at the thin line of troops and civilians they were to join—Major Potter's defense line—and quietly went to their assigned positions and began to dig in. They were still digging when the sun rose bright on the horizon.

"You lost the bet," Wallace said. "There's the sunrise."

Breckenridge thought for a moment, then said, "Well, I bet we never see it set."

With daylight, the men on Wake could see more clearly what they were up against, and the sight did not bolster morale. In every direction, completely ringing the atoll, Japanese ships slowly cruised in a circle out of range of Wake's guns. The count varied; Major Potter counted sixteen ships, Lieutenant Barninger at the five-inch battery on Peacock Point counted twenty-seven, others saw even more. But the actual numbers made little difference. Enemy ships were out there, and the marines couldn't touch them.

Then, at about 6:45, Lieutenant Kessler on Peale reported that three destroyers were closing within range of his guns. He opened fire on the lead ship and scored several hits before they steamed out of range.

Over the horizon, the Japanese carriers turned into the wind to launch their planes for a maximum effort strike against Wake. At 7:00 they roared over the islands, pouncing on anything that looked like a defensive position and giving wide berth to the areas defined by Japanese flags. Battery E at Peacock Point opened fire on the planes, a final gesture from the only remaining intact antiaircraft battery.

At the eastern end of the airstrip, Corporal McAnally's men were still holding off the enemy, though their position was becoming less secure by the minute.

"What the hell's that?" one of his men shouted as two figures slowly came toward them through the brush. They had large tanks strapped on their backs and were wearing goggles. None of the men had ever seen anything like it. It was one of the earliest uses of flamethrowers in the Pacific war.

"Looks like men from Mars," McAnally said, and he opened fire. He got one of them, but the other one threw himself behind a large chunk of coral. McAnally calmly lined up his sights on the center of the coral rock and started shooting. The steady stream of bullets chipped through the coral, shattering it, and the surprised Japanese was killed.

Everywhere McAnally and his men looked they saw more enemy soldiers massing for larger attacks. They would not be able to hold out much longer. Devereux could not afford to risk losing them, so he ordered the men to withdraw to Major Potter's line, which they were able to do without loss.

Meanwhile, at Battery E close to the lagoon, Lieutenant Lewis reported that his position was coming under fire. Mortar shells were falling on the airstrip not far away, and his men were being harassed by rifle fire.

Lewis sent out one gun crew of ten men under Sergeant Gragg along the road to the west. They had gone no more than fifty yards when they were pinned down by heavy fire. Gragg positioned his men to make a stand. At least they could try to keep the Japanese away from the antiaircraft guns.

At the tip of Peacock Point, the crews of the five-inch guns were also being fired on by mortars and machine guns. The battery commander, Lieutenant Barninger, took some of his men and formed a defensive line with two .30 caliber machine guns. With their backs to the sea, they waited for the enemy to come in force.

Further north, barely 100 yards in front of Devereux's command post, the thin line of Major Potter's unit was coming under fire. Potter could not hope to effectively cover the entire 850-yard width of the island at that point, not with the small number of men he had. He tried to cover the area from the airstrip to the beach, but even that distance stretched his force dangerously thin. Most vulnerable of all was a 450-yard gap of mostly cleared land along the runway between his line and the Battery E position. Potter realized the battery could be easily surrounded, so he sent out a squad, all that he could spare, to try to close the gap. They were no match for the larger enemy force, however, and were quickly driven back; two men were lost.

By 7:00, when Devereux reported to Commander Cunningham again, the situation was critical. The news was bad from all positions and growing worse by the minute. By all indications, Wilkes Island had fallen sometime before dawn. There had been no word from Lieutenant Poindexter's unit on the western end of Wake, and it was assumed to have been overrun. The Japanese were known to be on the northern side of the airstrip, beyond Putnam's small band and the three-inch gun it was defending. The airstrip had not been blown up, so it appeared that Kliewer's group had been taken.

The three-inch battery on the lagoon side of Wake and the five-inch battery at Peacock Point were both under fire, and the enemy was advancing against the last formal line of defense—Major Potter's force. If the Japanese broke through that line, there was nothing left to stop them from sweeping over the rest of Wake and onto Peale. Enemy planes were flying low over all three islands, bombing and strafing at will, and several ships stood by offshore ready to shell any part of the atoll at a moment's notice. There was no sign of hope.

Devereux reported all this to Cunningham, and the two men discussed the possibility of surrender. Clearly it had to be faced. All that the men on Wake could do was fight a holding action, buying time—at best a few more hours.

"Isn't any help coming?" Devereux asked.

"No," was the somber reply. "There are no friendly ships within twenty-four hours."

"Not even submarines?"

"Not even them."

Devereux paused for a moment, then said, "Let me see if there isn't something I can do up here."

"I tried to think of something—anything—we might do to keep going," Devereux wrote later, "but there wasn't anything. . . . We could keep on spending lives, but we could not buy anything with them."

As ranking officer, the decision was Cunningham's to make—a terrible, gut-wrenching choice that was to haunt him throughout the early months of his captivity.

There was a long silence on the phone, and then Cunningham made the decision to surrender. There could be no other.

"It was a numbing realization," Devereux wrote, "bitter to take, but Commander Cunningham's decision to surrender was inevitable, beyond argument."

"I'll pass the word," Devereux told him.

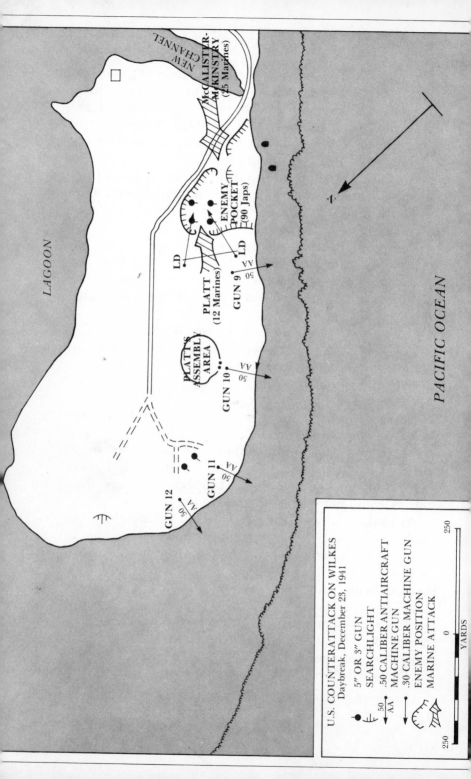

U.S. COUNTERATTACK ON WILKES
Daybreak, December 23, 1941

● 5″ OR 3″ GUN

SEARCHLIGHT

.50 CALIBER ANTIAIRCRAFT
MACHINE GUN

.30 CALIBER MACHINE GUN

ENEMY POSITION

MARINE ATTACK

250   0   250

YARDS

PACIFIC OCEAN

LAGOON

NEW CHANNEL

McCALISTER–
McKINSTRY
(25 Marines)

ENEMY
POCKET
(90 Japs)

LD

LD

PLATT
(12 Marines)

GUN 9

PLATT'S
ASSEMBLY
AREA

GUN 10

GUN 11

GUN 12

8

"The Death of Pride"

Devereux was wrong on two points in his assessment of the situation at 7:00 that morning—neither Wilkes Island nor Camp 1 had been captured. Indeed, in both places, the men were on the offensive, and they were winning, but there was no way that Devereux could have known.

By 4:00 A.M. on Wilkes, the Japanese were in possession of the three-inch gun emplacement of Battery F. They tried moving out of this position to the east, but the combined forces of Gunner McKinstry and Lieutenant McAlister kept them in place.

To the west of the enemy position, a lone machine gun emplacement, well camouflaged, kept up a deadly rate of fire. Several times the Japanese tried to sneak up on it, but each time they were flung back with heavy losses.

Captain Platt crawled for a half-hour through thick brush and coral to try to locate some of his men and to find out how the battle was going. Finally he reached a point close to the shore where he could see the three-inch position and the large enemy force there. They were well protected with riflemen and machine guns set up behind large coral rocks. Platt knew he was heavily outnumbered, but he realized that when daylight came the Japanese would find his isolated units and overrun all of Wilkes. He decided not to wait; he would attack first.

He made his way to a machine gun and ordered Platoon Sergeant Raymond L. Coulson to get the two .30 caliber machine guns and their crews from Kuku Point, along with the searchlight crews and anyone else he could find, and report back on the double. In less than a half-hour, Coulson was back with eight riflemen and the two machine guns and their crews. Quickly Platt briefed his men, and they filed out in the darkness to make their way to a point just west of the enemy position.

It was growing light by then, and Platt placed the two machine guns in a position where they could cover his eight-man charge. The gunners were told to fire short bursts, low to the ground, in order to avoid hitting the marines who were dug in beyond the Japanese position; Platt knew they were there because the Japanese were firing in that direction. Slowly the eight riflemen began to crawl toward the enemy. When they had gotten to within fifty yards of the enemy position, Platt's machine guns opened fire and the eight marines jumped to their feet and charged. More than ninety Japanese were in the three-inch gun position, but they were not expecting an attack from that direction.

Unknown to Captain Platt, McAlister and McKinstry were readying an attack from the east against the Japanese. Their combined force of fifty men started forward but was quickly stopped by a patrol of three Japanese well hidden behind a large rock formation.

McKinstry immediately started for the rock, but McAlister stopped him.

"Detail a man for that job," McAlister ordered.

Before McKinstry could protest, Corporal William C. Halstead spoke up.

"I got it, Gunner," he said, and he headed for the Japanese patrol while the rest of the men kept· up a heavy covering fire on both sides. Halstead scrambled up the front of the rock, and when he reached the top he shot all three Japanese.

McAlister and McKinstry decided to split their small force, with some of the men moving out to hit the enemy's flank while the rest pressed forward. McKinstry led the charge in the face of heavy enemy fire. He threw hand grenades as fast as his arm would move. Behind him ran two civilians passing the grenades to him.

Suddenly one of the Japanese casualties rose up in the midst of McKinstry's men and tried to bayonet one of the marines. He was cut down in a hail of bullets, and McKinstry yelled, "Be sure the dead ones are dead." Then machine gun fire pinned down the right flank of McKinstry's line, and he shouted, "Get going. Move on! You don't want to stay here and die of old age." The men on the flank leaped to their feet, overran the machine gun, and caught up with the rest of the line.

The Japanese were taking fire from three sides, and even though they were an elite group holding a strong position against an inferior force, they began to fall apart as a fighting unit. They took shelter wherever they could find it, abandoning their defensive positions. McKinstry saw a number of them in the ammunition bunker and threw in a hand grenade. He and Halstead rushed forward together and met a hail of bullets; Halstead was killed instantly.*

The marines rushed into the gun emplacement, and there were a score of individual hand-to-hand fights with rifle and bayonet. Corporal Robert E. Lee ran around the base of one of the ack-ack guns, and a Japanese soldier, thought to be dead, jumped up to face him. They each sprang forward, lunging with their bayonets. They missed and stared at each other for a

---

* After his retirement, McKinstry faced an armed robber across the counter of the liquor store he owned in San Diego, California. He shot the thief with his .45, surviving yet another battle.

fraction of a second, then lunged again. This time neither one missed, and they both fell dead.

When it was over, the Japanese had been wiped out, except for five who were seen running into the bushes with McKinstry close behind them.

"Bring back one alive, Mac," Platt shouted after him.

Captain Platt organized his men into raiding parties and sent them out to sweep the island in search of Japanese troops. There weren't any more, except for two wounded who were taken prisoner. They counted the Japanese dead on the island, and the toll came to four officers and ninety-four men. There were no other wounded; the marines had learned their lesson. American losses were nine marines and two civilians killed, four marines and one civilian wounded. Wilkes was securely in American hands.

Shortly after 7:00 A.M., dive bombers swooped low over the island strafing everything that moved. In between these attacks, Platt reorganized his defenses and turned his attention to the two prisoners. He wanted to find out if the Japanese intended additional landings on Wilkes. Using sign language, the two Japanese were interrogated and revealed that no more landings had been planned.

Platt worked frantically to restore communications with the command post on Wake. The marines could hear the sounds of fighting on Wake and see Japanese planes strafing and bombing, evidence that the battle was still going on. The only answer he was able to get on the radio was from Poindexter's unit at Camp 1, but they were out of contact with Devereux as well and could tell him nothing of the general situation.

Platt did the only thing he could do. He positioned his men and waited.

Across the boat channel, Lieutenant Poindexter was in good spirits. Though he was still out of touch with the rest of the island, he could hear the sounds of fighting and assumed that the rest of the marines, like his unit, were at least holding their own. His defensive line, arranged in a semicircle around the remains of Camp 1, had proven so strong that the Japanese had stopped trying to breach it. They made only occasional light probes looking for weak points, but they didn't find any.

By 8:00 A.M., noting that the enemy attacks were weakening, he decided to go on the offensive and head east toward the airstrip to try to link up with the forces on the eastern end of Wake. He detailed one of his men to search through the area and bring up every able-bodied man with a rifle that he could find. The first place to look was the Camp 1 bomb shelter, and the marine found it jammed with truck drivers, a searchlight crew, and supply personnel. He stood in the doorway of the shelter and said, "The lieutenant says for everyone with a rifle to move up to the line on the other side of the water tower."

There was silence. No one moved. Then a skinny eighteen-year-old supply clerk, Corporal Cyrus D. Fish, stood up and grabbed his rifle.

"What are we sitting on our asses here for?" he yelled, and he ran out of the shelter. Slowly the others moved, first one man, then another, then two more; they picked up their rifles and made their way outside, following Corporal Fish. There were twenty in all, and they walked slowly in the rubble of their former home to join Poindexter's force.

Poindexter looked around, pleased that he now had a unit of fifty-five men, and formed them into three squads. He gave orders to his noncoms, then pointed east.

"All right," he said. "Let's move out."

In his command post on Peale Island, Commander Cunningham gently placed the field telephone back in its holder and wondered what fate awaited them all at the hands of the Japanese. He looked around at the small group of men in the room, wanting to say something to them, but he couldn't. Dazed, he walked outside, pulled his .45 from its holster, and dropped it in a latrine. He got in his pickup truck and drove to the remains of the cottage where he had once lived, in another time. He rummaged through the debris and managed to shave and wash his face. Then he put on a clean blue uniform and drove south to surrender.

Shortly after Devereux put his phone down, Gunner John Hamas stepped inside the command post to report that the last of Captain Godbold's men from Peale had been placed on Potter's defense line.

"What are your orders now, sir?" Hamas asked.

Devereux looked at Hamas, a big strapping man who had been a marine for twenty years and a lieutenant in the Czech Army before that, and he sadly shook his head.

"It's too late, John," he said. "Fix up a white flag and pass the word to cease firing."

Hamas was shocked. He stared at Devereux in disbelief. Then the trained marine took over again.

"Yes sir," he said, and went out of the shelter.*

Devereux could hear him shouting to cease firing, his voice sounding like it would break.

"Major's orders!" Hamas was yelling. "We're surrendering. Major's orders."

Devereux ran to the doorway, his face thin and haggard, his eyes drawn and red. The sound of Hamas's words were too much for him.

"It's not my order, Goddamn it!" he said, though he

---

* Hamas voluntarily returned to Japan after the war to help in the search for war criminals. He committed suicide a few years later.

knew there was no other choice. The "death of pride" was hard for a marine to take.

One of the phone operators called to him, and he went back inside. It was Lieutenant Barninger's battery at Peacock Point asking for orders.

"Cease firing," Devereux said. "Destroy all weapons. The island is being surrendered."

He notified all the positions he still had contact with to do the same, and all over the island marines carried out his instructions. At the gun batteries, blankets were stuffed far down into the barrels and the guns were fired. Then hand grenades were dropped into the muzzles. Electrical cable was chopped into small pieces, and fire-control equipment smashed beyond repair. Twenty .45 caliber bullets were fired into the delicate height finder and director systems of each gun.

At Battery A at Peacock Point, Lieutenant Barninger told his men to eat as much of their food supply as they could before the Japanese came. Then he ran up a white flag, and the gun crews waited quietly for their captivity to begin.

At the command post, Sergeant Bernard Ketner paused inside the doorway and stared at the sad, dejected look on Devereux's face. He walked up to him and held out his hand.

"Don't worry, Major," he said. "You fought a good fight and did all you could."

He saluted smartly and left.

Lieutenant Lewis marched his men in formation from Battery E to the command post. Devereux was standing outside watching as Lewis briskly halted his unit.

"Sir," Lewis said, "the guns and fire-control equipment of E Battery have been destroyed."

Lewis reported in best military manner, displaying no emotion, but his men showed resentment and bewilderment as they stared at the white bedsheet nailed to a timber over the command post. They could hear firing from Potter's line. They had been told to surrender, yet marines were still fighting.

Devereux sensed what was running through their minds and tears ran down his cheeks as he spoke to them.

"I don't know whether any marines have ever surrendered before," he said, "but those are the orders and they'll be carried out."

Along the length of Major Potter's defense line, the word was passed from man to man. When it reached Breckenridge and Wallace, they recalled Breckenridge's earlier bets—first that they'd never see the sun rise, and second that they'd never see it set.

Wallace looked over at him and with a half-smile said, "Breck, I guess you're going to win that second bet."

They pulled the bolts from their rifles and threw them as far as they could into the undergrowth, then sat down to wait for the Japanese. Private First Class Wallace took out the last letter he had received from his girl. She said she was happy that he was in the Pacific where he wouldn't be in danger. Slowly he tore it into little pieces and let the wind take them from his hand. Neither man spoke as they watched the paper disappear. It was a last link with home and another life—and it was gone.

In front of the command post, Lieutenant Lewis's men sprawled on the ground resting, saying little. Finally, one marine asked the question on everyone's mind.

"What do you think the Japs will do with us?"

Sergeant Gragg growled, "If they don't shoot us, we'll probably go to Manchukuo and work in the salt mines."

"Join the marines and see the world," a young private said—"the hard way."

A few of them laughed, and one man got out a supply of chocolate bars he had been hoarding. He took one for himself and passed the rest around to his buddies. A

passerby might have thought they were a group of re-
cruits just back from a day of training, lounging in front
of the barracks, bantering, joking, kidding one another,
eating Hershey bars.

Major Devereux was concerned about the navy hospital, which was in a no-man's-land between Major Potter's
line and the Japanese. He tried getting through to it on
the phone, but there was no answer.

"Rig a white flag you can carry," he told the men in
the command post. "We'll have to go down there."

Sergeant Donald Malleck volunteered for the job, tied
a white rag onto a mop handle, and followed Devereux
outside. There was still shooting on the island, and Devereux did not know what they would meet, but reso-
lutely the two men marched south on the coral road.
Not far from the command post, a lone Japanese soldier
appeared. The marines stopped in the middle of the
road, and Malleck held the white flag higher.

Cautiously the Japanese came toward them, his rifle
held at the ready. He stopped a few feet away and
stared for a moment, then motioned with his bayonet.
Devereux followed the soldier's pantomimed instructions
and dropped his helmet and pistol belt on the ground
and emptied his pockets. The soldier looked through
Devereux's possessions and let him keep his wallet and
handkerchief. Sergeant Malleck did the same and was
forced to take his shirt off and leave it on the ground.

Walking a few paces behind the Americans, the soldier
motioned for them to walk down the road to the
Japanese line. A second soldier appeared, and just as
Devereux and Malleck approached him, a rifle shot rang
out and the soldier fell.

"The order has been given to cease firing," Devereux
shouted, "and damn it, you'll obey that order!"

The first soldier motioned for the two marines to walk

on. He knelt and rolled the body of the second Japanese over. When he saw that the man was dead, he stood and gestured down the road toward the hospital.

The Japanese force had taken the hospital before Devereux got there. They had flung open the steel door and fired inside wildly, killing one patient and wounding another. Then they herded everyone outside—sick, wounded, and able-bodied alike.

When Devereux and Malleck reached the hospital, they saw a dispiriting sight—about thirty Americans, many with dressings covering fresh wounds, sitting beside the road in four rows. Machine guns were trained at their backs. The men were wearing only shorts and shoes, and their hands were bound behind them with telephone wire. One end of the wire was looped around each man's neck in such a way that if he moved his hands at all, he would tighten the wire around his neck. It was the first indication of the kind of treatment they could expect from the Japanese.

As Devereux and Malleck were herded to the hospital entrance, they saw that several Japanese soldiers were watching them. One was wearing a sword, and Devereux asked him if he spoke English. The officer indicated that he did.

"Well, we are surrendering," Devereux said.

The officer smiled, said something in Japanese to those around him, and offered Devereux a cigarette.

"Where did you learn English?" Devereux asked.

"Studied at school," the man answered. "Also was at San Francisco World's Fair, 1939."

Just then there were cries and shouts from down the road. A group of Japanese had stopped Commander Cunningham's truck. As Cunningham approached them, the officer with whom Devereux had been talking looked from one American to the other in confusion.

"Who Number One?" he asked.

Devereux gestured to Cunningham. Then he suggested that he and Malleck go around the atoll to make sure everyone got the word about surrendering while Cunningham arranged the formalities.

Cunningham was searched and his wallet taken from him. He was put in the rear of the truck and driven off in the direction of Peale Island.

Devereux and Malleck, with an escort of twenty Japanese soldiers and the "World's Fair JG," as Devereux called him, started walking westward toward the airfield. It was 9:30 A.M., almost seven hours since Devereux had lost contact with some of his units. Now he would learn if they had survived the night.

The first position they came to was the three-inch gun that Lieutenant Hanna had used so well to shell the two destroyer-transports. Major Putnam and his group of marines and civilians had fallen back to the gun emplacement during the night to make a last stand. As Devereux and Malleck approached the position, they saw that the ground was littered with scores of Japanese dead.* The attackers had been forced back by the heavy defending fire to nearby airplane revetments, from which they could keep the marines pinned down.

Devereux made his way through curious, chattering enemy soldiers and climbed up on one of the revetments.

"This is Major Devereux!" he shouted. "The island has been surrendered! Cease firing! Put down your weapons!"

There was no answer from the gun emplacement, and Devereux yelled his instructions again. Still no one answered, and Devereux started to walk toward the position. A few marines stumbled out, Major Putnam among them. Dried blood covered most of his face.

---

* The Japanese lost at least sixty-two men trying to take Putnam's position.

"Jimmy," he said in a daze. "I'm sorry, poor Hank is dead."* And he told how Captain Elrod had been killed by a Japanese soldier playing dead.

Of Hanna's four-man crew and Putnam's twenty-two men of VMF-211 and twenty-two civilians, only ten men remained, and nine of those were wounded. Captain Tharin was the only man who had not been hit.** They had held out against an overwhelmingly superior force for six hours, without food or water, and with little prospect of survival.

Devereux watched the Japanese separate the officers from the enlisted men and take them all away. Sadly he turned and moved on to the next known position— Lieutenant Kliewer's. At 10:15, Devereux came within sight of the generator and called out to the men to surrender.

In the dugout, Kliewer and his three men watched warily as Devereux and Malleck, carrying the white flag, approached them. Groggy with exhaustion and hunger, they had been fighting off attacks all through the night and well into the morning, trying to repair the generator during the lulls. It still refused to start.

Devereux and Malleck came near, followed by a large group of Japanese, and the major called out again that Wake had surrendered.

In the dugout, a sergeant grabbed Kliewer's arm.

"Don't surrender, Lieutenant!" he said. "It's a hoax. Marines never surrender."

But Kliewer knew it was all over, and he ordered his

---

* Captain Elrod, who had fought so hard and so well in the cockpit of his Wildcat and on the ground, had been killed in the early morning hours. He stood up in the face of enemy fire to throw a hand grenade and was killed instantly.

** During the Korean War, Tharin's plane was shot down and he became a POW for the second time.

men to destroy their weapons. Wearily he led them out of the dugout and into captivity.

At the end of the airstrip, the crews of the two machine gun positions were taken, and the surrender party moved out toward Camp 1. Devereux and Malleck exchanged glances; there was rifle fire ahead, a lot of it. Someone was still fighting.

It was 11:00 A.M. Poindexter's group had been making good progress all morning. They were throwing the Japanese back with their three-pronged attack, and Poindexter figured that at the rate they were moving he would be at Peacock Point by dusk. Throughout the morning, Poindexter had counted enemy dead and so far had reached eighty. His men, fired by their success, were fighting boldly and well, and Poindexter felt that nothing could stop them. And then he saw a small group of men coming toward him. One of them was carrying a white flag. The Japs were surrendering, he thought.

As Devereux and Malleck drew closer to the fighting, some of the Japanese who had been battling Poindexter all morning turned and fired at them. About a dozen enemy soldiers jumped up and charged the two marines with fixed bayonets. The Japanese officer with the surrender party waved his sword and shouted at the troops. They put aside their bayonets, but they jostled the two men around, roughing them up. They thumbed through Devereux's wallet and threw everything away, including his only picture of his wife and son.

Poindexter shouted for his men to cover him and walked out to the center of the road. Black ointment, medication for flashburns, was smeared all over his face, and his pockets bulged with hand grenades. He wore a .45 at his hip and carried a Springfield rifle in one hand. As he got closer to the soldiers, his face split in a wide triumphant grin at the thought of his little group capturing so many prisoners.

Suddenly a familiar voice called to him.

"Drop your rifle."

Poindexter stopped in his tracks, stunned at the sudden turn of events. It was Devereux's voice, and now he could make out the slight figure of the major and another marine with him—they were the ones carrying the white flag.

The rifle slipped from his hands, and he walked forward. Devereux shouted to him again, and he unbuckled his pistol belt and let it fall. As Poindexter took the grenades from his pockets, some of the Japanese ran in terror. Carefully he placed the grenades on the road with their safety levers intact.

"Have your men stand up and leave their weapons on the deck," Devereux said.

From out of the brush, Poindexter's marines appeared, confused and hesitant. When the Japanese soldiers who had been falling back before these men all morning saw them, they yelled "Banzai" and charged with bayonets. The officer with Devereux stopped them just in time, and the marines were led away.

The party continued on, picking up isolated prisoners. As they reached the remains of Camp 1, a potentially explosive event occurred. A small group of newly captured prisoners was with Devereux as they passed the American flag flying from the water tower (it had been placed there after the flagpole had been destroyed).* The Japanese soldiers saw the flag and began to yell, and one of them started up the ladder to the top of the tower. Devereux looked around at his men and saw their anger and frustration. He could see that some of them were watching the Japanese, eying their rifles.

---

* There is no record of when the flag was placed atop the tower, or the circumstances under which it occurred.

"Hold it!" Devereux said. "Keep your heads, all of you!"

The men stood in place, glaring as the Japanese soldier cut the flag down.

Out of sight of Devereux and his men, Sergeant David Rush calmly lined up the Japanese in the sights of his machine gun. Somehow, just as he was about to fire, he saw Devereux and the white flag. He eased his finger off the trigger, took the firing pin from his weapon, and threw it as far as he could into the water.

Near the Wilkes boat channel there was another marine who hadn't seen the surrender party. He was sitting in his dugout behind a .30 caliber machine gun, wondering what was happening on the rest of the island. Suddenly a Japanese plane passed low overhead. Gunnery Sergeant John Cemeris was a crack shot, and he grinned as he watched the line of tracers reach out and hit the plane. Smoke poured from it, and there were angry murmurs from the Japanese surrounding Devereux and his group of unarmed marines. Devereux and Poindexter ran in the direction of the firing.

"Stand up," Poindexter yelled. "Put your hands over your head."

When the group reached the western end of Wake, Devereux pointed to the barge in the center of the channel and told the World's Fair JG about the dynamite charges it contained. Communications had been cut off before Devereux had been able to order it blown up, and he didn't want to risk an accidental explosion now, not with his men at the whim of the Japanese.

Standing at the water's edge, Devereux assumed that his job of notifying all units of the surrender was finished. To his surprise, the Japanese officer motioned him to the boat dock and told him they were going to Wilkes to arrange the surrender of the island. Devereux was astounded—it was the first he knew that Wilkes had won its battle.

Platt's men had spent a watchful morning on Wilkes, ridding the island of the few Japanese still alive and preparing for the next attack. Japanese planes swooped over the island most of the morning strafing and bombing. Around noon, lookouts called Platt to report that a destroyer was moving closer to the shore near the channel and that other ships—including three transports—were also beginning to move in. Landing boats were sighted heading toward the channel.

Platt phoned Lieutenant McAlister and told him to man the five-inch battery and fire on the boats, but when the crews reached the guns, they found both of them irreparably damaged by the morning's air raids. Platt rushed to the battery to examine the guns himself. A few minutes later he inspected the three-inch guns and found them permanently out of action also.

There was nothing to do but allow the enemy landing craft to land and meet the troops on the beaches. He rounded up all his men and two .30 caliber machine guns and started toward the boat channel to what many men thought would be their last battle. They were too exhausted to withstand another major attack, and they knew this would be larger than the last one. But they were determined to do the best they could with what they had.

While Platt's men were marching toward the channel, Devereux and Malleck, with thirty Japanese soldiers, landed on the eastern end of the island. Devereux took a few steps on the sand and then shouted, "This is Major Devereux! The island has been surrendered! Put down your arms!"

There was silence. Offshore the landing craft were getting closer, but that was the only movement to be seen. There was no sign of life on Wilkes. The surrender party started walking inland, and Devereux saw a flash from a destroyer's guns. Seconds later a shell burst at the edge of the beach, then another one even closer.

Devereux and Malleck looked at each other, then at the World's Fair JG, and continued walking. Both marines thought it would be prudent to take shelter, but as long as the Japanese officer didn't do so, they wouldn't either. They were both scared, Devereux wrote, but they weren't going to admit it to the enemy.

Finally when a shell exploded less than fifty yards away, the officer told everyone to take shelter and ordered a signal sent to the destroyer to cease firing.

Meanwhile, Platt's force was making its way across the island. It was slow going, the men were tired, and planes kept harassing them. In one such attack, Private First Class Robert L. Stevens was killed—the last marine to fall in combat in the battle for Wake. At 1:30, a rifleman called back to Platt, "Somebody's coming down the road."

Platt gestured for the men to take cover. They waited in the brush, weapons aimed at the road. Platt saw a white flag but thought at first it was a trick. Then he heard Devereux's voice.

"The island has been surrendered. Don't try any monkey business."

The surrender party walked steadily onward, still seeing no one. Then Platt's dirty and disheveled men started to come out from hiding. They looked sullen and distrustful. They didn't advance; they just stood there, rifles at the ready, facing Devereux and the Japanese behind him.

Captain Platt walked forward to salute the major.

"We have surrendered," Devereux told him.

Platt stared at him, his mouth grim and tight. For a moment, there was a strained silence.

"Yes sir," he said, and he turned around and ordered his men to lay down their arms.

Platt's men and the surrender party walked on to the bitterly fought-over three-inch gun emplacement. The Japanese became very excited when they saw how many of their fellow soldiers had been killed. At his command post, Platt released the two Japanese prisoners. The Japanese troops from the landing barges joined them, and the marines were herded back to the channel and transported across to Wake.*

The officers were driven to the Japanese headquarters located near Lieutenant Hanna's three-inch gun emplacement on Wake. Devereux and the others were given some canned food, the first time most of them had eaten since 6:00 the previous day. He ate listlessly. He was exhausted from the ordeal of the past two weeks and was beginning to realize the enormity of what had happened to them. He felt "dead inside."

As he sat there dazed and bewildered, overcome with despair, he saw some of his men being marched toward him. Most no longer had their uniforms, and some were even barefoot, limping painfully from the sharp coral. Their shoulders were bent, and they shuffled along with their heads down. They were a sorry-looking lot.

At the head of the column was Sergeant Edwin F. Hassig, a large barrel-chested man, every inch the recruiting poster image of a marine. Hassig saw his commanding officer up ahead, and he turned and bellowed to the men behind him.

"Snap outta this stuff! Goddamn it, you're Marines!"

And when they marched past, it was as a fighting unit of leathernecks. To Major Devereux, they were the smartest-looking marines he'd ever seen. It was a sight he would never forget.

---

* Platt, whose nickname was "Cutie," was later killed in the Korean War.

9

"The Unknown Lay Ahead"

Throughout that long, painful, and humiliating first afternoon of captivity, there was one thought in the minds of most men on Wake—the relief force that was due the following day. That afternoon, and for the next several days, the men looked out to sea hoping and praying for signs of the Pacific Fleet, but all they saw were enemy ships lying peacefully at anchor. The Japanese seemed to take no steps to protect themselves. Cargo ships were moored to buoys off the Wilkes channel, and Commander Cunningham was amazed that the Japanese made no attempt to maintain blackout conditions on the island.

All the men could do was stare at the peaceful scene offshore and wait for American ships and planes to appear over the horizon. They occasionally talked about what the Japanese might do to them when the attack came, but they spent more time planning how they could help once it started.

One day they heard gunfire. It was unmistakable; their deliverance was at hand.

"This is it!" they yelled, and braced themselves for any reprisal measures the enemy might take. But it was the Japanese testing some new guns they had brought to the island.

As each day turned into the next, their hopes diminished. They talked less and less about it and finally came to the despair-filled realization that there would be no relief, no rescue. They knew they had been written off, and the future they faced was death or an unknown number of years as prisoners of war.

They were right; they had been written off. The task force had been recalled just two and a half hours before Wake surrendered, when it was only twenty hours sailing time from the atoll. In the early morning hours of the twenty-third, while the battle was raging on Wake and Wilkes, Cunningham's dispatch notifying Pearl that the enemy was landing was handed to Captain Charles H. McMorris, operations officer on the CincPac staff. He at once notified Admiral Pye and his chief of staff, Rear Admiral Milo F. Draemel, and the three men met to consider the situation.

For several hours they argued back and forth over what they should do, weighing each option in terms of the ultimate consideration: the safety of what remained of the Pacific Fleet. Before they were able to reach a decision, Cunningham's second dispatch was received.

They read it—"Enemy on island, issue in doubt"—and fell silent for a moment. Each man knew what was behind the words; it was too late to do anything about Wake. America desperately needed a victory, and Ad- hours, not once the Japanese were on the beaches.

But there was still the question of what to do with Fletcher's Task Force 14. Should they continue to Wake and attack the enemy ships there? In eight hours they would be close enough for the *Saratoga's* planes to reach Wake. America desperately needed a victory, and Admiral Pye knew how much the navy needed one to restore its morale, shattered along with its battleships. But what were the chances of winning, they wondered. Could they risk an engagement with an enemy force of unknown strength? Could they risk a second naval disaster just two weeks after Pearl Harbor?

At 9:11 on the morning of the twenty-second (the twenty-third on Wake), Admiral Pye reached his decision. It was too risky; the task force would be recalled.

On the bridge of the *Astoria*, Admiral Fletcher read the dispatch and announced to his staff, "We're called back to Pearl Harbor."

The officers were shocked at first, then angry and indignant. Tempers flared, voices rose. Some of the staff pleaded with Fletcher to ignore the orders and make a fast run for Wake with those destroyers that had enough fuel and attack any ships they could find. He refused, and bitter words were exchanged. The atmosphere on the bridge was tense; some called it mutinous. Rear Admiral Fitch, who wanted to press on, was so angry that he left the bridge.

In the ready room of the *Saratoga*, the marine fliers, anxious to go to the aid of Putnam and Tharin and Elrod and the others—they knew most of them—cursed aloud, and some broke down in tears.

On the decks of the *Tangier*, the marines of the landing force were busy stowing away loose gear and rechecking their weapons. It was rumored that the Japanese were readying another attack on Wake. Charts and maps were reviewed, and excitement grew as the ships sailed on. During the early afternoon, some marines were taking a break—leaning on the ship's rail, staring at the sea—when they noticed something wrong. The *Tangier's* shadow on the water was in the wrong direction. They had reversed course—they were sailing away from Wake. The news spread quickly from one end of the ship to the other. A few minutes later, the officers passed the word that they were being recalled.

Shortly after reaching his decision, Admiral Pye sent a dispatch to Admiral Stark in Washington.

"The use of offensive action to relieve Wake had been my intention and desire. But when the enemy had once landed on the island, the general strategic situation took precedence, and the conservation of our Naval Forces became the first consideration. I ordered the retirement with extreme regret."

The American public was not told of the aborted attempt to relieve the beleaguered garrison at Wake. But in barracks and officers' clubs around Pearl and on the bridges and wardrooms of ships at sea, men of the navy and Marine Corps knew—and they felt anger and shame and impotence.* The marines on board the *Tangier* were sent to Midway, another "spit-kit of an island," where they wondered if they would end up like their brothers on Wake.

A few days later, American forces all over the Pacific, from Pearl Harbor to Bataan, heard the voice of Tokyo Rose taunting them.

"Where, oh where, is the United States Navy?" she asked.

She was not the only one to ask that question.

The civilians and the enlisted marines on Wake quickly learned how brutal their captors could be. As they were being marched to a central point on the island, several groups passed wounded Americans crying out for help. The Japanese disregarded them and would not allow the prisoners to pick them up. They could only walk by helplessly and hope that somehow the wounded would be taken to the hospital.

---

* When General Pfeiffer was interviewed in 1968 by the USMC Oral History Unit, he said of the recall of the relief force, "I call this the blackest day in the history of the U.S. Navy." He described the atmosphere at Pearl Harbor at the time as being "decidedly negative and defeatist." When Admiral Joseph M. Reeves, former commander in chief of the United States Fleet, learned of the recall, "he regarded it as a disgrace to the United States Navy."

Virtually all the marines were marched to the two hospitals, and there the nightmare began. All of them, able-bodied and newly wounded alike, had their hands trussed tightly behind them with the wire looped around their necks. Their hands were pulled high up on their backs, causing excruciating muscle pains, but if they tried to lower their hands, the wire cut into their necks.

The men were prodded with bayonets and shoved into the two concrete shelters used as hospitals without food or water. Those who were pushed in first found themselves pressed against the walls as more men were jammed in after them, packed tightly against one another "to the point of suffocation," according to Gunner Hamas. It became so crowded that there was barely room to stand. Some men passed out and fell against others who could do nothing to help as unconscious hands pulled the nooses tight.

The air grew close and foul; men became sick and vomited on each other. The wounded moaned, and blood flowed from their untreated injuries. Gunner Hamas managed to make his way to the entrance, determined to get help, at least for the wounded. Hamas was an old China hand and remembered some Japanese words from his days in Shanghai.

He looked out the entrance and saw an old Japanese officer not far away. He knew he was risking a bayonet, but he called to him, asking him to free Dr. Kahn so he could look after the wounded.

The officer listened to Hamas's halting phrases in Japanese and replied in English.

"You doctor, too?"

"No sir," Hamas said.

"Are you an officer?"

"Yes sir," Hamas answered.

The elderly Japanese ordered the guards to untie Hamas and Dr. Kahn, and he gave them each a few cigarettes. Kahn went to work immediately, but there was little he could do except save those who were unconscious from strangling themselves.

An hour or so later the Japanese officer came back to the dugout, and Hamas decided to see what else he could do. He held up his hands and pointed out how swollen they had become from being bound so tightly. The officer agreed to let Hamas loosen the wires on the other men and later said they could remove the wires altogether.

Little by little, Hamas was able to get other concessions. Some of the men were allowed outside, and Hamas was able to collect discarded clothing from the area to distribute among the prisoners. While he was doing this, one of the guards became annoyed and jabbed Hamas in the hip with his bayonet.

Finally the marines were herded out of the dugouts and taken with the civilians to the airstrip. Most of them had no clothing, and when a chilling wind blew up that night, they scooped out shallow holes in the tightly packed coral with their bare hands and burrowed in them in an effort to keep warm. They remained out in the open without food or water for fifty-four hours.

The wounded were taken to a damaged building where they had more room but nothing else. The Japanese had taken the remaining medical supplies for their own wounded. They didn't care whether the American wounded lived or died.

The marines at the airfield had to work hard the next day clearing away debris and collecting and burying the dead. They had not eaten since before their capture, nor had they been given any water. Finally food was brought out to the airfield, but the Japanese deliberately left it in the sun to spoil within sight of the prisoners before they were allowed to have any of it. They were given water from gasoline drums, and they gagged and retched as they tried to force it down their parched throats.

About thirty of the men, including Gunner Hamas and Captain Tharin, were detailed for the grisly job of burying the American dead. Under heavy armed guard they roamed over Wake and Wilkes picking up bodies. Some of the dead had been stored in the reefer, but the refrigeration equipment had been destroyed. By the time the burial detail got there, the bodies had begun to decompose. The stench was overpowering, and when the men came out, they were pale and gasping for fresh air.

Inside they found several large jars of maraschino cherries, which they wolfed down on the spot despite the putrid odors. They knew the Japanese would take the jars away from them if they brought them outside, and so they ate them within sight of the decaying corpses. Four years later, when Gunner Hamas got back to the United States, the taste of cherries would make him violently ill.

A large trench four feet deep was dug near Lieutenant Hanna's three-inch gun position, and the bodies were placed in it. Rubber ponchos were laid across them, weighted with heavy chunks of coral, and the men stood by the fresh mound of earth for a moment while one of them said a prayer.

Most of the officers fared better; they did not suffer the brutalities the Japanese displayed toward the enlisted men. Commander Cunningham was placed in the reasonably intact guest cottage along with Captain Platt, Captain Wilson of the army radio team, and Mr. Hevenor of the Bureau of the Budget. Guards kept constant watch on the men and for the first two days gave them no food whatsoever.

The men set to work to make the damaged cottage more habitable, sweeping out the broken glass and fallen plaster. One of them found some canned goods placed there during the fighting. They rationed them, not knowing how long it would be before the Japanese would feed them.

In the cottage next door, Major Devereux, Dan Teters, Major Putnam, and seven others were confined. Any contact between the men in the two houses was strictly forbidden.

Late that afternoon Admiral Kajioka, resplendent in his dress white uniform, wearing his ribbons and his sword, came ashore to formally take possession of Wake in the name of the Emperor of Japan. It was given a new name—Otori Shima, or Bird Island—and Kajioka handed Cunningham a proclamation.

PROCLAMATION

Here it is proclaimed that the entire islands of Wake are now the state-property of the Great Empire of Japan.

PUBLIC NOTICE

The Great Empire of Japan who loves peace and respects justice has been obliged to take arms against the challenge of President Roosevelt. Therefore, in accordance with the peace-loving spirit of the Great Empire of Japan, Japanese Imperial Navy will not inflict any harms on those people—though they have been our enemy—who do not hold hostility against us in any respect. So, they be in peace!

But whoever violates our spirit or whoever are not obedient shall be severely punished by our martial law.

Issued by
THE HEADQUARTERS OF
JAPANESE IMPERIAL NAVY

The Americans found it "interesting" reading, but they were more concerned with food. Christmas dinner for the men in Major Devereux's cottage consisted of crackers washed down with evaporated milk. By the third day of captivity, however, the Japanese began to serve food to the officers—mostly stews accompanied by bread, tea, and sugar. The food was brought to the cottages by enlisted marine prisoners under the watchful eyes of the guards. With one of his meals, Devereux found a note which gave him the first indication of the kind of treatment his men were receiving. He immediately dispatched a formal note of protest to the Japanese commander and settled back to await his reaction. There was no predicting it; conditions might be made more unbearable because of the protest, but Devereux was compelled to try. He never received an answer, but he learned later that the lot of the enlisted men improved shortly after his note and they were being fed better.

Cunningham, Devereux, and the other officers were interrogated almost every day of their stay on Wake, but they were never asked for secret information or subjected to pressure or torture. The men considered most of the questions asked of them to be terribly naive, even foolish.

"How did you know the war had begun?" was the first question the Japanese asked Devereux.

"We got a message from Pearl Harbor," he answered.

"How did you know we were going to attack Wake?"

"We didn't know."

"Didn't you know our planes were coming?"

"No."

"Well, how did you know they were coming?"

"We didn't know until they arrived."

"Didn't you have any detection apparatus? You know what I mean."

Finally, the interrogator came out with what was on his mind—radar.

Two weeks after the island's surrender, Admiral Kajioka's chief of staff asked Devereux to show him where the big guns were located. Devereux showed him, but he wasn't satisfied. He was convinced that there were larger guns hidden on the island because he could not believe that so few guns had done so much damage to the ships of the first invasion force. All the other officers were asked the same question, and apparently the Japanese never were convinced that there were not more guns cleverly hidden from view.

Commander Cunningham was asked about the American plan for war in the Pacific. The Japanese referred to it by its official designation (WPL-46), which led Cunningham to believe that the enemy had broken American codes. This concern was reinforced when one of his interrogators boasted openly that they had indeed broken the codes.

During one of these interrogations, Cunningham noticed that the uniform of one Japanese officer was badly torn and held together with safety pins. When asked what had happened, the man replied in an affable tone: "You shoot my ship."

Through these initial days of captivity, Cunningham began to notice differences among the Japanese guards, and he came to realize that a prisoner could not hate all his captors equally. Some stood out as being much more humane and decent than others. One young sailor was particularly friendly, and he told Cunningham he was worried about his parents, who lived in Hawaii; he feared the Americans would kill them.

"You think they all right? Please?" he would ask, and when reassured, he would clap his hands together. "Pretty soon war over," he said. "Everybody shake hands."

Cunningham had a long discussion with a highly cultured naval officer who displayed no hatred toward his American enemies, nor was he elated over the early Japanese successes. He spent a lot of time trying to convince Cunningham that Japan had been morally right to launch a war against America.

"Japanese," he said, "are fair people. They want only

human justice. America is trying to strangle Japan."

Then he asked a question that Cunningham was to hear many times in the years to come.

"Did you send the message saying, 'Send more Japs'?"

Cunningham told him that he had not sent it, but he did not think the Japanese believed him.

The officer smiled at Cunningham and said, "Anyhow, it was damned good propaganda."

The enlisted men were sent out on work details every day and found that they were able to take some measure of revenge against their captors by committing highly dangerous acts of sabotage. Shortly after the surrender, the Japanese gathered up the rifles and machine guns from all over the atoll and put the marines to work cleaning them. They did so; the outsides of the weapons shone to perfection and would have passed the most rigorous inspection. But when the guards weren't looking, the marines poured salt water down the barrels so that the rifles could not be fired.

A group of marines was sent to clean the still serviceable three-inch antiaircraft guns. They spent hours polishing the guns until they looked brand new, then put gritty sand into the recoil mechanisms. Machine guns shone with a luster, but vital inner parts disappeared into the undergrowth.

And so the days continued into the new year of 1942, the enlisted men working every day and the officers undergoing pointless interrogations. When they were not being questioned, the officers read and played cards, washed their clothes, and were sometimes allowed to take short walks, always under guard.

On January 11, more than two weeks after their capture, the situation suddenly changed.

"You will soon be taken to a safer place," an officer told Cunningham, and the next day at noon the men were told to be ready to leave within the hour. The announcement was met with dismay. Life on Wake, while tedious and hard, was at least predictable. Routines had been established, ways of dealing with their captors worked out, even semi–cordial relations established the some of the guards. A way of life had evolved which, while not the most desirable, offered one advantage: it was known. A private or an officer knew what he could and could not do, how much he could risk, what he could get away with.

But now that would all change. They were going to a new place with new guards, new rules to be learned by the slow and sometimes painful trial-and-error process. The familiar world of Wake Island would soon be behind them; only the unknown lay ahead.

10

"Not Just Any Island"

Wake Island, like the Americans who defended it, spent the next forty-five months in the backwash of the Pacific war. Wake had become more of a graveyard than a Japanese bastion when the atoll changed hands again in 1945. In an ironic reversal of positions, the Japanese on Wake found themselves written off, expendable, as America launched its program of island-hopping victories. The front line, if there could be said to be any such thing in the Pacific war, quickly moved away from Wake in the direction of Japan, and the Japanese on the atoll were increasingly isolated.

It was bypassed in the American drive westward but not ignored. Heavy bombers—B-24s—raided the island repeatedly, major carrier strikes roared over again and again. Heavy ships poured well over 7,000 five-inch and six-inch shells into the sand and coral. In a five-month period in early 1944, almost 1,000 sorties were flown against Wake, dropping over 1,000 tons of high explosives. The Japanese went underground into their own shelters—and those built by the marines—and huddled in choking darkness as the earth heaved and tumbled about them.

As the war continued, their lifeline to Japan was squeezed almost shut; by June of 1945 the last supplies reached the island, and they had to be brought by submarine. No Japanese surface vessel could survive the long voyage through what had become an American ocean. The submarine was able to deliver only half its supplies before roving American planes forced it to submerge. By the summer of 1945, the Japanese on Wake were running out of everything—ammunition, food, medicine, spare parts. All they could do was wait in their bunkers for the next air raid and stare anxiously out to sea for the inevitable invasion fleet!

Lance Corporal Watanabe Mitsumara kept a diary of those terrible days on Wake. Food and bombs were the major items of concern. American planes flew overhead 243 of 268 days, but it was the lack of food more than the constant bombing that sapped the Japanese garrison's strength.

The diary tells of eating tree leaves and "grass dumplings." Men died almost every day from starvation. Morale and discipline broke down and increasing numbers of soldiers were arrested for stealing food. At one time, as many as seventy men were in prison, reduced to a diet of a little "gruel, rice, and salted soup"; prison was a death sentence.

On March 17, 1945, Corporal Mitsumara completed his diary with the words, "Praying to God to have more food." He died from malnutrition.*

The Japanese paid a heavy price to take and keep Wake—more than twenty times the American casualties. During the sixteen days it took them to capture the atoll, the estimated enemy losses were 820 dead and 1,153 wounded, and this is a conservative estimate (the Japanese do not have accurate casualty information for

* Excerpts from a translation of the diary were sent to Admiral Cunningham, in 1968, by Master Sergeant Charles R. Jackson, USAF, who was stationed on Wake in 1963.

that period). Between the time they captured Wake and their surrender of it, they lost 600 more men to the bombing and shelling raids. But even more deadly were malnutrition and disease, which claimed 1,288 lives. Thus, a total of 2,708 Japanese soldiers died there. In addition, when it was still possible for ships to get through to Wake, they evacuated 974 wounded and seriously ill men to Japan. By the time the war ended, 405 troops—a third of the remaining Wake force—were ill, half of them bedridden. It was an enormous price to pay for less than four square miles of what turned out to be totally useless territory. The possession of Wake did nothing to prevent or even slow down America's march across the central and western Pacific. The wall that Japan had hoped to erect across the Pacific turned out to be made of paper, easily pierced by the hundreds of new ships that replaced those on the bottom of Pearl Harbor.

On September 4, 1945, the American navy appeared again off the coast of Wake, but it was not the invasion fleet the Japanese had so long expected. There were only three ships—the destroyer-escort *Levy* and two others. They were small ships and lightly armed, and they came not to invade but to occupy. The war was over; Emperor Hirohito had surrendered two weeks before. The shooting and killing had stopped; only formalities remained.

At 7:45 A.M. on September 4, a small and much battered whaleboat flying a white flag eased its way through the Wilkes channel. A mist shrouded the atoll, and the coxswain gingerly threaded the boat through the opening in the reef and headed toward the *Levy*. Sitting stiffly on a wooden bench seat, the Japanese commander of Wake, Admiral Shigematsu Sakaibara, was coming to meet his American conquerors to formally sign the surrender document. With him were three aides and the commander of army forces on Wake, Colonel Shigeharu Chikama, and his aide.

The small boat pulled alongside the *Levy,* and with Admiral Sakaibara in the lead the Japanese came aboard. They talked for several minutes with American officers, and then Marine Brigadier General Lawson H. M. Sanderson appeared. Unsmiling, he curtly nodded to the Japanese to take their places around the green felt-covered table set up on deck. Four photographers and two movie cameramen crowded around the table to record the scene.

After a few questions on technical matters, General Sanderson handed Admiral Sakaibara a pen and two copies of the surrender document, one in English and one in Japanese.

"We must guard against sabotage," General Sanderson said.

"There need be no worry," Admiral Sakaibara replied. "None of our men has the strength for such action." He explained that their meager rations were enough for only seventeen more days.

Later that morning a boat pulled away from the *Levy* and headed toward Wake. It carried a marine officer and a group of correspondents. As the boat neared the shore and edged its way through the channel, the officer's eyes swept over the island, checking what he saw against the scenes imprinted in his memory. Faces and voices came back to him as the boat nudged against the dock, and he half expected to see a battered Wildcat, its engine sputtering, climb from the end of the runway, or a group of khaki-clad marines drinking beer in the officers' club.

What he did see were two Japanese soldiers standing at attention, saluting him as he stepped off the boat. Major, now Colonel, Walter L. Bayler was back on

Wake. The last American to leave before it was captured, he was the first to return.

Bayler and the correspondents commandeered a Japanese truck and set off to tour the island. One of the few recognizable structures was the water tower near what was once Camp 1. The steel framework was rusty, and the tower leaned slightly on only three of its legs. Next to the tower was the old flagpole, its base choked with wild scrubby bushes, its shaft bent and unsteady.

As the party wandered over Wake, Bayler pointed out places where the marines had lived and fought. There was not much left: two sticks were all that remained of the headquarters building. A row of smashed toilet bowls indicated where the bachelor officers' quarters had been under construction when the war began. The underground hangar, where Lieutenant Kinney and Sergeant Hamilton restored planes from wrecks, was still in use. On the other side of the airstrip were three gaunt and broken Wildcats, partly covered by weeds and bushes. American equipment and machinery were strewn everywhere. The marines' Springfield rifles were neatly stacked at the dock. Construction equipment, some of it still in use, was scattered all over the atoll.

The graves of the defenders of Wake were still there. There were forty-nine marines buried on Wake, plus three sailors and seventy civilians, all killed in the sixteen-day battle for the atoll.* But Bayler found another grave there, too—a long trench dug two years after the island's surrender. The white paint on the posts and markers was not quite dry, the bushes around it freshly trimmed, obviously in anticipation of an occupation force.

The grisly story came out later at one of the many war

---

* Of the 400 marines who were taken into captivity, 376 were still alive by the end of the war. Thirteen men were known to have died during the years of imprisonment, leaving eleven still unaccounted for.

crimes trials held throughout the Pacific. In January 1942, when the defenders of Wake left for POW camps, about a hundred construction workers were kept behind to work for the Japanese in building up the island's defenses. Dr. Shank, the civilian doctor, stayed as well. The men worked hard with little food and no prospect of escape, and they huddled in bunkers for the second time in their stay on Wake—only this time the bombs that exploded around them were American.

The raids grew heavier. Surface ships lobbed their massive shells, and the Japanese became convinced that the construction workers were in radio contact with the American navy, directing their planes to the island. On the night of October 7, 1943, the Japanese rounded them all up, tied their hands tightly behind their backs, blindfolded them, and led them down to the beach on the north side of Wake. They were placed in a line, a very long line, facing the machine guns. No one survived.*

On the day Americans returned to Wake, its 1941 garrison was celebrating its release from almost four years of captivity. Most of the men were still in prison camps, but the treatment had improved immensely with the Japanese surrender. American planes flew over the camps in Japan dropping supplies, and representatives of the Red Cross visited. "Every day was Christmas," Devereux wrote. While they waited for American land forces to reach them, the prisoners took over the administration of the camps. They received food and medical aid from the Japanese, and one night ·at the camp on the island of Hokkaido, where most of the Wake marines had recently been sent from China, the

---

* Admiral Sakaibara and eleven of his officers were later tried and sentenced to death for this crime.

Japanese gave a dinner party for Devereux and the other officers.

Food and wine were lavished upon the former prisoners, men who for years had subsisted on a near-starvation diet. The Japanese were gracious, bowing and smiling at the Americans, many of whom had at one time or another been beaten unconscious at the whim of a Japanese guard. The sadism, brutality, and indifference of the last forty-five months were replaced by laughter and obsequiousness.

The senior Japanese officer rose to propose a toast to "everlasting friendship between America and Japan." All of the Japanese smiled and nodded. The Americans exchanged glances, but no one said a word. Finally a marine captured in North China in the first days of the war—Major Brown—slowly stood up. The Japanese became quiet, smiling at him, awaiting his reply. His eyes darted from face to face, from the haggard, gaunt looks of his fellow officers to the round, beaming faces of his enemies. His words came out taut and sharp, cutting through the artificial atmosphere in the room.

"If you behave yourselves," he said, "you'll get fair treatment."

Fair treatment was a lot more than the survivors of the fight for Wake received after they were taken off the atoll. Indeed, life in prison camps in China and Japan made the two weeks of captivity on Wake seem mild by contrast.

The men had been hauled aboard a ship in cargo nets and dropped on the deck. They were forced to run through a gauntlet of yelling sailors who hit them with clubs and fists. Then they were packed inside cold bare steel rooms containing nothing except straw pallets. They were fed twice a day, smaller amounts than at any time during their imprisonment—a bowl of rice and water, a tiny scrap of fish, sometimes with two olives and a strange-tasting radish.

Every evening the prisoners lined up in rows for inspection, and anyone who failed to carry out a command immediately was cuffed sharply across the face. Since most of the men knew no Japanese and the guards knew no English, the marines were frequently struck. Captain Platt was pulled out into the passageway and beaten severely with a club for talking too loudly.

Six days later the ship docked at Yokohama, and some of the men were brought up on deck to pose for photographs and to answer reporters' questions. Eight officers and twelve men, including Majors Putnam and Potter, Lieutenant Kliewer, and Commander Keene, were taken off the ship and sent to a POW camp in Japan.

"So long, we'll be seeing you one of these days," they yelled to the others, and then they were gone.

On the voyage from Japan to Shanghai, in China, five men were taken from the cargo hold and led away.* The guards blindfolded them, tied their hands behind their backs, and took them up to B deck. There Lieutenant Toshio Saito, commander of the guards detachment, stood on a box. One hundred fifty members of the ship's crew and the guards formed a silent semicircle around him. Next to him, five of his men stood at attention; each one held a large sword.

The Americans were brought forward, and Saito took a piece of paper from his pocket and read to them in Japanese. "You have killed many Japanese soldiers in battle. For what you have done you are now going to be killed—for revenge. You are here as representatives of your American soldiers and will be killed. You can now pray to be happy in the next world—in heaven."

---

* They were Seaman First Class John W. Lambert, Seaman Second Class Theodore D. Franklin, Seaman Second Class Roy J. Gonzales, Master Sergeant Earl Raymond Hannum, and Technical Sergeant William Bailey.

The Americans stood bewildered and frightened. They did not understand what Saito had said and had no idea what was happening. Then they were made to kneel on the deck. A Japanese sailor who was in the crowd described what happened.

"The sword as brought down on the neck of the first victim made a swishing noise as it cut the air. As the blade hit and pierced the flesh it gave a resounding noise like a wet towel being flipped or shaken out. The body of the first victim lay quietly, half across a mat and half onto the wooden deck."

Four more times a sword flashed through the air. The bodies were mutilated and thrown overboard.*

Bleak and barren isolation, freezing wind whistling through ramshackle barracks, rice so thick with tiny pebbles that men broke their teeth, dawn-to-dusk work, beatings, exhaustion, boredom—such phrases, while accurate, cannot fully describe life at Woosung prison camp, a few miles outside of Shanghai.

The guards were cruel and totally indifferent to human suffering. Beatings were common. A man could be clubbed unconscious for the least infraction of a rule, or sometimes just at a guard's whim. The worst offender, the most sadistic of them all, was Isamu Ishihara, a civilian interpreter who took great delight in flogging, kicking, and beating helpless men. The prisoners called him the "Beast of the East," and he was the most hated man at Woosung.

But even more wearing than the cold, the bad food, and the beatings, were the emotional consequences of being a prisoner serving an indeterminate sentence. What does it do to a man to be told, as the Wake

---

* Four of the five executioners were sentenced to life imprisonment after the war. The fifth was acquitted. The men were paroled nine years later. Saito, who survived the war, was never apprehended.

marines were, "From now on, you have no property. You gave up everything when you surrendered. You do not even own the air that is in your bodies. From now on, you will work for the building of Greater Asia. You are the slaves of the Japanese."

Abandonment in a tiny corner of the earth, separation from all semblance of a normal life, worry about their families—all served to sap the spirit, to reduce morale and hope to nothing. When would it end? Would they ever see their wives and children again, or would they die where they were, forgotten, pushed aside into the farthest reaches of their loved ones' memories, erased by time?

In Woosung, as in scores of other POW camps, the spirit was often under greater stress than the body, and the Japanese made every effort to strip the men of their pride and self-respect, to make them feel like slaves. There was, as Major Devereux put it, a never-ending "war of wills for moral supremacy," with the Japanese trying to break the men's spirit and the Americans trying desperately to hang on to every shred of self-respect. To the men of Wake it was a battle just as important as the one they had waged on their lonely atoll. In the prison camps, as on Wake, they fought back with everything they had, making do, improvising, enduring on will and determination alone.

In order to help win this battle against the Japanese, Major Devereux insisted on maintaining military discipline to the same degree as would have been practiced in the United States. It made the men feel as though they were still part of something, still maintaining a code and way of life of their own, independent of what the enemy tried to impose on them. They were prisoners— hungry, ragged, cold, and exhausted—but they were marines, with all the fighting spirit and pride that the corps had always stood for.

In December 1942, after a year of captivity, the prisoners of Woosung were marched five miles to another camp at Kiang Wang—"the worst hellhole of our captivity," Major Devereux described it. The men worked twelve hours a day, six days a week, building a rifle range. Under the supervision of the interpreter Ishihara, they were driven so brutally that their health, precarious enough to begin with, was more seriously affected. Tuberculosis, dysentery, malaria, and influenza ravaged the prisoners, and they lost so much weight that many became little more than walking skeletons. At the same time, the Japanese instituted the most severe period of interrogation the men experienced during the whole of their captivity. More torture and beatings were the rule.

Day followed day, week followed week, month followed month in a timeless blur of hunger, cold, pain, and misery—1942, 1943, 1944—meaningless numbers on a calendar that recognized no date as different from any other. Night, and the chance to sleep four men to a bunk huddled together to keep warm, was the goal. Survive another day, one day at a time, one step at a time, one watery bowl of rice at a time. Survive. Remain a human being in the midst of the inhuman. Remember, you're a marine! Survive—because one day it will end. One day it has to end!

It was not until the spring of 1945, more than three years after their capture, that the end seemed to be in sight for the survivors of Wake. On a clandestine radio made by Lieutenant Kinney, the men were getting word of what was happening in the outside world, of how the ring was closing around the Japanese. They had seen huge new bombers—B-29s—high overhead, bombing Japanese installations around Shanghai as early as the winter of 1944, but the most exciting and hope-filled development occurred one day in the spring of 1945.

Army P-51 fighters passed so low over the camp that the men could wave to the pilots. Their presence meant only one thing; an American air base was not too far away. For the first time their spirits soared, and they whistled and laughed as they went about their work.

Allied forces were indeed getting closer, so close that on May 9, 1945, the prisoners were herded into boxcars for a five-day trip to Fengtai, where conditions were more primitive than anything faced before. Then, a month later, there was another crowded boxcar for a four-day trip to the port of Pusan in Korea, where they were forced to walk three miles in heavy rain and mud. A new prisoner, a pilot with only one leg, hobbled along with the rest of them on makeshift crutches. He would have been bayoneted had he dropped out.

For three days they stayed in Pusan, where the flies swarmed all over them and the food was like garbage. Then a ship—twelve hours jammed together below decks —for a voyage that was still harder to bear that took them to Japan, the main island of Honshu. There they were herded into coaches, 170 men in cars designed to hold 88, and they rode north, passing mile after mile of bombed-out rubble.

On July 6, their journey ended on the island of Hokkaido, their last prison camp. The enlisted men were sent down into mines to work twelve to fourteen-hour shifts. The officers worked in a lumberyard.

And suddenly it was over.

"Very soon we will all be friends again," a Japanese guard said one day.

The defenders of Wake had survived.

Two men of the Wake garrison reached home earlier than the others. On the night of May 10, 1945, five officers jumped from a boxcar into the night while traveling at a speed of forty miles an hour. Two of the officers were North China marines, one was a Flying

Tiger, and two were from Wake—First Lieutenants Kinney and McAlister. They all survived the jump and were found by Chinese communist guerillas. For forty-seven days they made their way through Japanese-held territory, covering a distance of 700 miles by foot, horse, and boat. By July of 1945, a month before Japan's surrender, they were back in the states.

Another Wake Island prisoner escaped from the Japanese—in fact, he did so twice. On the night of March 11, 1942, less than two weeks after the prisoners had arrived at Woosung, Commander Cunningham, together with Dan Teters, a British officer, and a Chinese boy interned with them, burrowed beneath the electrified fence and got away, but they were captured the next day. They were all taken to Shanghai, where they faced a court-martial on the charge of deserting the Japanese army. They were tried once, and then again, and Cunningham and the British officer were each sentenced to ten years in prison. Dan Teters received a two-year sentence, and the Chinese boy one year.

Two years later, Cunningham courageously escaped again, only to be recaptured the next day and to face another court-martial—his third. This time he received a life sentence and was sent to Nanking's Military Prison. Two weeks before the war ended, he was transferred to a jail in Peking, and on the day of Wake's surrender to the Americans, he was on a plane headed for home.

The new flagpole on Wake was a half-mile away from the battered rusty one that had been in use in 1941. Forty Japanese troops were lined up on one side of it facing a small group of United States Marines and thirty sailors. Everyone stood rigidly at attention. Brigadier General Sanderson read the surrender proclamation out loud.

"Prepare to raise the colors," he ordered. It was 1:43

in the afternoon, September 4, 1945.

Master Technical Sergeant Ralph Broc and Private First Class Millard Moore stepped forward smartly and began to raise the American flag. Nearby a bugler sounded the crisp, clear notes of To the Colors.

The Americans and the Japanese saluted as the flag caught the breeze. Offshore the *Levy* fired a twenty-one-gun salute while General Sanderson formally turned the island over to the navy.

Commander William Masek, USN, spoke very briefly, but his words indicated what the heroic defense of this tiny atoll meant to the American people.

"I accept this island proudly, because this is Wake Island. Not just any island. It was here the Marines showed us how."

Epilogue

Wake Island was not the last defeat or the biggest; there were more to come. In the newspaper headlines of the early months of 1942, new names would take the place of Wake—Singapore, Bataan, Corregidor, Java. But the spirit of the siege of Wake lived on. A defeat, yes, but to many it was a victory because it showed Americans what they could do. "Remember Wake!" became the new slogan in the arsenal of words that were the only weapons the country had in strength as 1941 turned into 1942. It helped to forge the spirit and determination that carried the fleets, the men, and the planes from one island to another island and finally to a surrender ceremony in Tokyo Bay.

For a short time, it restored for Americans something that had been shattered with the ships of the Pacific Fleet—pride and confidence in themselves. It was an example of bravery to be followed in the long months and years ahead. And it was accomplished by a handful of men: 449 marines, 68 sailors, 6 soldiers, and a few hundred civilian construction workers. They did it with four outdated fighter planes, cannon from old battleships, and a small number of machine guns and rifles, wearing helmets of World War I vintage. But most of all they did it with the kind of lean, hard courage, aggressiveness, and imagination that many people thought Americans had lost. In those grim, dark days at the end of 1941, they showed us what could be done, what the American people had the ability to do.

In one of the last messages to leave the island, the

commander of the marine fighter squadron summed it up. "All hands have behaved splendidly and held up in a manner of which the Marine Corps may well tell."

Appendix I
Wake Island Unit Citations Given By President Roosevelt

The White House
Washington
5 January 1942

Citation by
THE PRESIDENT OF THE UNITED STATES
of

The Wake detachment of the 1st Defense Battalion, U. S. Marine Corps, under command of Major James P. S. Devereux, U. S. Marines

and

Marine Fighting Squadron 211 of Marine Aircraft Group 21, under command of Major Paul A. Putnam, U. S. Marines

The courageous conduct of the officers and men of these units, who defended Wake Island against an overwhelming superiority of enemy air, sea, and land attacks from December 8 to 22, 1941, has been noted with admiration by their fellow countrymen and the civilized world, and will not be forgotten so long as gallantry and heroism are respected and honored. These units are commended for their devotion to duty and splendid conduct at their battle stations under most adverse conditions. With limited defensive means against attacks in great force, they manned their shore installations and flew their aircraft so well that five enemy warships were either sunk or severely damaged, many hostile planes shot down, and an unknown number of land troops destroyed.

Appendix II
The Cunningham Controversy

The publication of Admiral Cunningham's book in 1961 made public a controversy which had been kept within the confines of the military. The controversy, reflected in the title of the book, *Wake Island Command,* centered on Cunningham's charge that his role as commanding officer on Wake had been ignored. Wake Island became identified in the public mind as strictly a Marine Corps operation, and Devereux received all the recognition as the hero of Wake, while Cunningham's role was not noticed at all. One can understand how, to a career officer, such a lack of recognition could be a vital concern.

Hanson W. Baldwin, former military editor of the *New York Times,* noted in his book, *The Crucial Years: 1939-1941,* that "Plain Navy Department ineptitude and confusion (many key personnel did not even know Commander Cunningham was on the island, much less in command, until the battle was over), plus the tendency of the Marines to move into publicity vacuums, created the impression that Devereux, not Cunningham, commanded at Wake."

In his early months as a POW, Cunningham reported that he was extremely depressed because of his feeling of responsibility for the surrender of Wake—a decision which, as we have seen, was his and his alone to make as senior officer present. He feared that if he survived the war he would face a court-martial for that decision, and he worried that his family would be disgraced by it.

He need not have worried. When he returned to the states, he learned very quickly, "how ironic my concern had been. So far as the public was concerned, I had made no decision at all.

"To most of my countrymen, in fact, I did not even exist."

He learned then, for the first time, how the defense of Wake had developed into a massive Marine Corps legend. As he read the newspaper and magazine accounts of Wake from those early weeks of the war, he saw that Devereux was considered the commander of Wake. There was not a single reference to the fact that a naval officer had been in overall command of Wake—or even on the atoll in any capacity.

Mrs. Cunningham, who knew her husband was on Wake, became increasingly alarmed during those early weeks of the war. In all the communiqués and articles there was no mention of her husband.

On January 5, 1942, President Roosevelt issued a unit citation to the defenders of Wake, naming Devereux and Putnam as the commanding officers of ground and air activities respectively (Appendix I).

Two weeks later came the first official recognition of Cunningham's existence. Japanese radio reports broadcast in the United States noted that among the prisoners from Wake was Commander Cunningham, commander of the atoll. A day or so later, the Navy Department announced that it could not confirm that a Commander Cunningham had been on Wake when it fell.

Through the intervention of Senator Robert M. LaFollette, Jr., contacted by Mrs. Cunningham, the navy did admit that Cunningham had indeed been on Wake in charge of all naval activities. The next day, however, newspapers carried the statement from the Navy Department that Devereux had been in command of the Wake Island force.

On March 14, 1942, the navy awarded both Devereux

and Cunningham the Navy Cross, but again the honor of command was bestowed upon Devereux. A year later, in response to Mrs. Cunningham's campaign of letter writing, she received the following from President Roosevelt's naval aide.

"The Navy Department advises me that Commander Cunningham arrived at Wake Island a short time before that Island was attacked by the Japanese. His presence on Wake was not known to the Navy Department during the early part of the action there. It has been recognized, however, that he was the senior officer present there and acknowledgement has been made of that fact."

But that changed nothing; Devereux remained the commander of Wake in the eyes of the world at large. That was strongly reinforced in the summer of 1942, when Mrs. Cunningham learned of the filming of the movie *Wake Island* and arranged for a private screening. Walter Abel played the role of Cunningham, but in the film he died after the first bombing raid, and the Marine Corps major played by Brian Donlevy took over the command. Mrs. Cunningham protested that this was not "as accurate and factual as possible" a presentation as the producer of the film had claimed. The producer countered with the information that the navy and the Marine Corps had approved the script. Mrs. Cunningham tried legal action, but since the navy had no objection to the film, her protests were ineffective. The picture became a big success and helped greatly with recruiting drives and war bond sales.

In April 1943, the *Saturday Evening Post* began a series on Wake, a now-it-can-be-told story written by then-Lieutenant Colonel Walter Bayler. The series was tied in with the publication of Bayler's book *Last Man Off Wake Island*. Mrs. Cunningham read the first installment in the *Post*, then the second, and was horrified to see no mention whatsoever of her husband. Finally, in the third and last installment, in the description of the mass burial, this line appeared: "Spiv Cunningham, who was in charge of naval affairs on the island, was there."

Mrs. Cunningham wrote a great many letters during the war in an effort to right the wrong she felt had been done to her husband. When Cunningham returned home in 1945 to find he was the "forgotten man of Wake," he too, with some reluctance at first, became involved in trying to change the way history had recorded the event.

In 1947, Devereux published his book *The Story of Wake Island,* parts of which were serialized in the *Saturday Evening Post* under the title "This is How It Was." At first Cunningham was delighted with what he read.

In the first article, Devereux clearly stated that it was Cunningham and not he who was commander of Wake, but from then on, Cunningham was less than satisfied. Cunningham wrote: "And from that point on the role of Spiv Cunningham in the defense of Wake degenerated to virtually nothing.

"Throughout a sixteen-day battle, to all intents and purposes, Cunningham had been huddled in the barracks or busy in the command post. . . .

"I appeared as a virtual noncombatant who emerged from the shadows just in time to force the shocked Marines to surrender."

Also in 1947, the official Marine Corps history, *The Defense of Wake,* was published, written by Lieutenant Colonel Robert D. Heinl, Jr., and again Cunningham felt that he had been slighted. Not consulted or interviewed for this official history, he wrote that it "throughout presented me, where I was named at all, as a sort of bystander, active if at all in a housekeeping capacity."

"The realization that again, and this time in an official account, I had been denied any real share in Wake's defenses except the humiliation of surrender filled me with the greatest sense of outrage I had yet experienced."

Feeling that his reputation and future military career were being jeopardized, Cunningham continued his attempts to set the record straight in official circles by lodging a formal complaint with the Navy Department at the advice of Fleet Admiral Chester Nimitz. He collected statements from other officers and wrote a lengthy account of the defense of Wake. Among his points of evidence were two interesting statements. Dan Teters wrote: "I have never seen any legitimate grounds for Devereux getting such a hell of a play. You were in command, Keene was your second, and I could never see where that point was open to argument." Lieutenant John Kinney wrote: "Cdr Cunningham was senior officer on the Island and he actually exercised command. Major Devereux was in charge of the defense of the island but took his orders from Commander Cunningham. It was Commander Cunningham who ordered the surrender. Usually the top man gets credit in a military operation, but this case seems to be different."

Cunningham's complaint and supporting material made their way up the chain of command to Admiral T. L. Sprague, chief of naval personnel, who recommended that Cunningham officially be given equal credit, along with Putnam and Devereux, for the defense of Wake. Sprague also recommended that a corrected Presidential Unit Citation be given to the Wake defenders under the command of then-Commander Cunningham.

At the next step in the chain of command, Vice-Chief of Naval Operations Admiral A. W. Radford noted that Cunningham's role as commanding officer of Wake should be recognized officially, but he did not recommend a new and changed unit citation. His reason was that the original citation could not be corrected because it had been issued by a president who was no longer living.

When Cunningham retired from the navy in 1950, he wore at the ceremony, "with some bitterness," the Presidential Unit Citation ribbon given in the name of two of his subordinates for a command he had held. There was one final official rebuff. In 1953, a ceremony was held to mark the reburial of the Wake dead in a military cemetery in Honolulu. Devereux and others were invited, but Cunningham did not even know about the ceremony until several years later.

Other more informal reminders occurred throughout the years. Whenever a discussion turned to "Where were you during the war?" Cunningham heard, "You were on Wake? Then you were with Devereux?"

Admiral Cunningham has, in my opinion, every reason to feel aggrieved at history's lack of recognition of his role as commanding officer on Wake. For whatever reason, deliberate or accidental, the press as well as the Navy Department bestowed all the recognition and credit on General Devereux, clearly identifying him as the atoll's commander. Cunningham's role—indeed, even his existence—was not recognized during the war. It was only after the war, and then only as a result of Cunningham's own efforts, that his position was established. By then, however, it was too late for any public recognition; the words "Devereux" and "Wake Island" had become inexorably linked in the public mind.

This is a highly personal tragedy for Admiral Cunningham, one understandably difficult to accept passively, which is why he went to such lengths to correct the official record. He was on Wake, he was the ranking officer, he had to accept the responsibility for the decision to surrender, yet he received no recognition. He shared equally in the dangers, but unequally in later reward. His two attempts to escape from prison showed a high degree of courage in risking death, certainly as much as displayed by anyone on Wake. On the wide and jarring canvas of the whole war, Cunningham's personal tragedy is insignificant, but in the life of a career military officer it is a catastrophe of dramatic proportions.

It should be noted that nowhere does Admiral Cunningham attempt to detract from the heroism displayed by General Devereux and the other defenders of Wake, nor does he depict himself as solely responsible for directing the stand. "I wanted no credit as a mastermind of Wake's defense," he wrote.

As a naval officer, he would not be expected to be familiar with ground fighting at the tactical level. Clearly that was Devereux's province and area of competence, just as fighting in the air was Putnam's area of responsibility. Indeed, it would have been highly presumptuous of any naval officer in that situation to have tried to tell an experienced marine officer how to disperse his troops or where to place their weapons, and the like. A navy officer is not trained in such matters. For him to attempt to personally direct the actions of the marine garrison in the details of their fighting would be like Devereux telling Putnam's pilots how to go about attacking an enemy formation. There are many situations in war in which the senior officer present must allow a subordinate officer to make tactical decisions, when such decisions lie in that subordinate's area of expertise.

Therefore, credit for the details of the conduct of the land and air battles for Wake must go to those trained for such operations, Devereux and Putnam—which it did. But to totally ignore the role of Cunningham as the man charged with the overall responsibility for everything that happened on Wake would be a gross injustice to the man—which it was.

It should also be noted that General Devereux has never publicly commented on the controversy. When questioned about the matter in 1970 by the Oral History Unit of the United States Marine Corps Historical Reference Section, and in 1975 in my interview with him, he said that there was no difficulty in the command relationship between himself and Cunningham "because . . . actually he'd never been trained for anything like this, base defense, and he had no, well, knowledge about how to operate." He also reiterated that Cunningham's decision to surrender "without question was the correct decision to make."

The final chapter of the Cunningham controversy was written on September 29, 1976, from the Oval Office of the White House. At the instigation of Mr. Leonn D. Boone (and with the assistance of the author), Congressman Garry Brown of Michigan initiated an investigation of the matter and requested the president to issue a new Unit Commendation including Admiral Cunningham's name.

President Ford's response, in a letter to Admiral Cunningham, follows.

THE WHITE HOUSE

WASHINGTON

September 29, 1976

Dear Admiral Cunningham:

My staff has been corresponding with Representative Garry Brown and Senator Bill Brock during the past several months regarding the omission of your name from the Presidential Unit Citation of forces defending Wake Island during the Japanese invasion of December 1941.

As you are aware, the original Presidential Citation of forces participating in the defense of Wake Island was issued on January 5, 1942, by the late President Franklin D. Roosevelt to: "The Wake detachment of the 1st Defense Battalion, U.S. Marine Corps, under command of Major [James] P. S. Devereux, U.S. Marine Corps, and

Marine Fighting Squadron 211 of Marine Aircraft Group 21, under command of Major Paul A. Putnam, U.S. Marine Corps." This issuance occurred one month prior to the formal establishment of the Presidential Unit Citation by Executive Order, No. 9050, which authorized the Service Secretaries to award the citation to United States military units for outstanding performance in action on or after October 16, 1941.

Since that time such awards cite only the units involved and do not include the names of any individuals. I believe that such a practice is appropriate inasmuch as the Presidential Unit Citation is a unit award, not a personal award citing individual actions or heroism.

The Commander in Chief of the Pacific Fleet recommended on October 2, 1943, that the original Presidential Unit Citation be amended to include the "Navy and Army personnel present" during the siege of Wake Island. This recommendation was forwarded by the Secretary of the Navy to President Roosevelt, who modified the citation as recommended.

Since the original citation was issued before procedures for awarding the Presidential Unit Citation were clearly established, it appears that the citation was written at the personal direction of President Roosevelt. Although the omission of your name is not considered to be a deliberate action, history does not provide us with specific circumstances under which the citation was issued or the reasons President Roosevelt chose to word the citation as he did. In view of the fact that the citation was personally signed and issued by the late President Roosevelt, and because it is current policy to cite only the units involved and not to include the names of any of the personnel, the citation cannot be withdrawn or modified.

The story of Wake Island has been carefully documented since the end of World War II. Although you were not cited by name in the Presidential Unit Citation issued by President Roosevelt, the Department of the Navy and many historians, including civilian writers, have given you full credit for being the Officer in Charge of Naval Activities at Wake Island during the siege. This is also reflected in your official service record. Additionally, you were awarded the Navy's second highest personal decoration, the Navy Cross, for your heroic efforts in defense of Wake Island.

Our Nation recognizes your courageous leadership in defense of Wake Island as a major contribution toward building a lasting structure of freedom and peace in the world. In this our bicentennial year, it is indeed appropriate to stop and reflect upon the contributions of Americans like you. Your devotion to the principles upon which our country was founded is deeply appreciated not only by me, but by all our fellow Americans who enjoy the freedom and independence which you fought so valiantly to preserve and protect.

Please accept my deep expression of gratitude and admiration, as well as my personal best wishes.

Sincerely,

GERALD R. FORD

Appendix III
The Survivors

The Wake Island survivors' association, called "The Defenders of Wake Island," meets every June in Oklahoma City, Oklahoma. These successful reunions have been organized by Jack Skaggs since 1960. The group's quarterly newsletter, the *Wake Island Wig-Wag*, is published by Franklin D. Gross, 2225 South Overton, Independence, Missouri 64052.

Space does not permit a summary of the activities of all Wake Island personnel since the war, but the reader may be interested in the careers of the major figures mentioned in the book.

REAR ADMIRAL WINFIELD SCOTT CUNNINGHAM

Promoted to captain after his return to the United States, Cunningham was sent to Pensacola, Florida, where Commanders Keene and Greey were also assigned. Cunningham commanded a seaplane tender in the Pacific, and at a Navy Day celebration in Japan in 1946, his Annapolis class ring, taken from him early in captivity, was returned. It had been recovered from the home of Toshio Saito, commander of the guard on the ship that had taken the American prisoners from Wake. In 1947, Cunningham was given command of the Naval Air Technical Training Center at Memphis, Tennessee. He retired in Memphis in 1950 and still plays a very good game of golf.

In 1962, Cunningham was invited by the FAA to participate in the dedication of Pan American Airways' new terminal building on Wake Island. He found the atoll greatly changed—a 10,000-foot runway, an 8-lane bowling alley, concrete barracks, and neat rows of homes for 1500 military, Pan Am, and FAA personnel. He discovered two gun emplacements on Peacock Point and the monument to the Wake Island defenders. Partly overgrown by brush, this simple tribute consisted of an engine cowling and broken propeller taken from one of the last Wildcats to fly in the battle for Wake, supported by a pile of coral. Two wooden signboards described the battle.

BRIGADIER GENERAL JAMES P. S. DEVEREUX

Devereux's return to the United States was marked by a tumultuous hero's welcome in Maryland and the gift of a new Buick. He was promoted to colonel, sent for refresher training to Quantico, Virginia, and assigned to Camp Pendleton, California, with Colonel Potter as his executive officer once again. Devereux retired from the Marine Corps in 1948.

Beginning in 1951, Devereux was elected to four terms in the United States Congress, where he devoted most of his efforts to the House Armed Services Committee. During a round-the-world congressional trip, he visited Wake Island and saw much that was familiar. The wreck of the destroyer-transports still hung on the reef offshore, and his old command post was intact. In Japan, the congressmen were given a dinner by Japanese officials, and Devereux was asked if he had ever been in Japan before. "Yes," he replied, "as a guest of the Emperor!" On a stopover in North Africa, he found Dan Teters, who was working on a navy construction project. The naval engineer in charge was Commander Greey, who had held the same position on Wake.

Devereux served as Director of Public Safety in Maryland after his retirement from Congress, and today lives on his farm, Wexford, in the beautiful Green Spring valley north of Baltimore. He breeds and shows horses, and still rides frequently.

BRIGADIER GENERAL PAUL A. PUTNAM

After repatriation in 1945, Putnam took a leave of absence to regain the thirty pounds he lost during imprisonment. He attended the Field Officers' School at Quantico, Virginia, and the Air War College at Maxwell Field, Alabama. The command of a fighter group at Cherry Point, North Carolina was his next assignment, followed by duty at the Pentagon as Chairman of the Intelligence Committee of the NATO Standing Group. At the Marine Air Station at El Toro, California, he commanded a fighter group and later became chief of staff of aircraft, Fleet Marine Force, Pacific. His last assignment was as Marine Corps representative on the Medical Evaluation Board. He retired on a thirty percent disability for partial deafness, caused by "too many guns, bombs, engine exhausts, and sonic roaring of propeller blades."

Putnam lives in Fairfax, Virginia, on the outskirts of Washington, D.C., where his activities today consist of "doing almost everything I want to—and, so far, of not doing anything I don't want to . . . a very pleasant way of living." He takes frequent fishing vacations in the North Carolina mountains.

BRIGADIER GENERAL GEORGE H. POTTER

Potter's Annapolis class ring was recovered along with Admiral Cunningham's. Potter retired from the Marine Corps in 1948 and spent several years in business, including five years as a field service engineer with Boeing Aircraft. He now lives in Daytona Beach, Florida, where he enjoys golf and fishing.

BRIGADIER GENERAL WALTER L. J. BAYLER

Bayler was the only man to serve in three "hot spots" in the early days of the war—Wake, Midway, and Guadalcanal. During his months on Midway he received a great many letters from relatives of the men on Wake and went about the "somber business" of answering them all. He served in the navy's Bureau of Aeronautics, Electronics Division, attended the National War College, and commanded the Third Marine Air Wing. After his retirement in 1957, he worked as a field service and support engineer for Hughes Aircraft. Bayler also taught high school physics for ten years and now lives in Santa Ana, California.

Notes

The subtitle of the book was suggested by an article in *Time* of January 19, 1942 entitled "Flame of glory: Wake's hopeless, gallant fight." The opening quotation is from the book, *Zero,* co-authored by Commander Masatake Okumiya of the Japanese Imperial Navy. The quotation was selected by Franklin D. Gross for the masthead of the *Wake Island Wig-Wag,* the newsletter of the Wake Island survivors' association.

CHAPTER 2   *"To Deny Wake to the Enemy"*

Morison, *The Rising Sun in the Pacific,* discusses the military plans for winning a war in the Pacific (pp. 33-34). The story of the *Burrows* and its voyage to Wake is told by its captain, Ross Dierdorff, in "Pioneer party—Wake Island," *United States Naval Institute Proceedings,* April 1943, pp. 499-508. The letter from Admiral Kimmel to Admiral Stark of April 18, 1941 is reported in Heinl, *The Defense of Wake,* p. 1; Morison, *The Rising Sun in the Pacific,* pp. 226-227; and Sherrod, *History of Marine Corps Aviation in World War II,* p. 35. The order from Admiral Stark to Admiral Kimmel of June 23, 1941, "Establishment of defensive garrison on Wake Island," is reprinted in Hough et al., *Pearl Harbor to Guadalcanal,* p. 98.

CHAPTER 3   *"Do the Best you Can"*

See Devereux, *The Story of Wake Island,* for the description of taking leave of his family in January 1941 (pp. 40-41), his meeting with Colonels Pickett and Pfeiffer (p.

39), the cables to Pearl regarding the use of civilians for military construction (pp. 31-32), the stopover on Wake Island of Saburo Kurusu (p. 28), his remark that improvisation was the "basic industry" of Wake (p. 36), and his comments on morale during the last weekend before the war (pp. 39-40). The quotation about Major Devereux ("He's the kind of guy who would put all the mechanized aircraft detectors into operation and then station a man with a spyglass in a tall tree.") is from *Newsweek*, January 5, 1942. See Cunningham, *Wake Island Command*, for his description of his assignment to Wake Island and his arrival there (pp. 20-31), his remark on the inadequacy of the three-inch guns (p. 35), and his comment about the last week of peace (p. 49). See Bayler, *Last Man Off Wake Island*, for his description of the camouflaged gun emplacements at Peacock Point (p. 23), his comment on the arrival of the Wildcats (p. 27), and his letter to his wife of December 6, 1941 (p. 30). For a discussion of the defense battalion concept see Charles L. Updegraph, Jr., *U.S. Marine Corps Special Units of World War II*, Marine Corps Historical Reference Pamphlet, 1972, pp. 61-77. See Toland, *The Rising Sun*, for a discussion of Admiral Yamamoto's naval plans (p. 213). See Toland, *But Not in Shame*, for information on Admiral Halsey's activities and his meeting with Major Putnam (pp. 9-10); see also Major Putnam's letter to COMAG-21 of December 3, 1941, in Hough et al., *Pearl Harbor to Guadalcanal*, p. 101. The weekend of December 6-7, 1941 on the home front is reported in Lingeman, *Don't You Know There's a War On?*, p. 19, and Hart, *Washington at War*, p. 5.

CHAPTER 4   *"This Is No Drill!"*

See Devereux, *The Story of Wake Island*, for the account of his activities on the morning of the attack on Pearl Harbor (pp. 42-46), his receipt of the news from

Lieutenant Lewis of the attack on Wake (pp. 50-51), the wounding of Lieutenant Conderman (p. 52), his remark about Mr. Hevenor's lack of punctuality (p. 58), his comments about the first raid (p. 55) and about "getting underground" (p. 66), and the bombing of Camp 2 (p. 69). See Cunningham, *Wake Island Command*, for his description of the failure to allow the Chamorros on the Pan Am Clipper (p. 63), the number of civilians who assisted the military (p. 284), the messages from Pearl Harbor (pp. 68, 78), and the situation by December 10 (p. 82). See Bayler, *Last Man Off Wake Island*, for his remarks on the flag raising (p. 33), and the first air attack (p. 38). The quotation about the Japanese pilots waggling their wings to signify "BANZAI" is from Heinl, *The Defense of Wake*, p. 15. The Japanese report on damage to fourteen planes during the raid is cited in Heinl, p. 17. The information on Wake's air raid alarm system is from Hough et al., *Pearl Harbor to Guadalcanal*, p. 111. The origin of the Sea-Bees is described in Baldwin, *The Crucial Years*, p. 477.

CHAPTER 5 *"Send Us More Japs"*

See Devereux, *The Story of Wake Island*, for the account of the attack on the *Yubari* and the crash of Captain Elrod's plane (pp. 80-90). The Marine Corps axiom, "Maybe you oughta get more . . .," is from Devereux, p. 96. See Cunningham, *Wake Island Command*, for the messages from Pearl Harbor (p. 93), and for his "Send us . . . more Japs" cable (p. 109). The quotation from Admiral Kajioka is from Heinl, *The Defense of Wake*, p. 22.

CHAPTER 6 *"When Time Stood Still"*

Both Hough et al., *Pearl Harbor to Guadalcanal*, p. 122, and Heinl, *The Defense of Wake*, p. 30, note that the survivors' postwar recollections of the period from December 12-20 are extremely confused, sometimes hopelessly so. See Devereux, *The Story of Wake Island,* for his account of the period "when time stood still" (pp. 104-105), the remark that "you wouldn't die today" (p. 103), the bomb near the command post (p. 103), the messages from Pearl (p. 136), the conversation with Captain Elrod (p. 132), the letter to his wife and son (p. 136), and the anecdotes about Corporal Brown (p. 102), Sergeant Gragg (p. 120), Private First Class Wallace (p. 120), Corporal Richardson (p. 121), and Sergeant Cain (p. 123). See Cunningham, *Wake Island Command,* for his description of the time of "attrition" (pp. 98-99), the sighting of a submarine (p. 107), his messages to Pearl Harbor (p. 105), and his letter to his wife and daughter (p. 114). See Bayler, *Last Man Off Wake Island,* for the account of his belief that reinforcements would be sent (p. 113), and his departure from Wake (pp. 134-136). See Heinl, *The Defense of Wake,* for the quotations from Lieutenant Kinney about the Japanese bombing and from Major Putnam about the airplane mechanics (p. 33). The relief force is discussed in Heinl, "We're headed for Wake," *Marine Corps Gazette,* June 1946, pp. 35-38. The Japanese records on the loss of their submarines are reported in Hough et al., *Pearl Harbor to Guadalcanal,* p. 122.

CHAPTER 7   *"There Are Japanese in the Bushes"*

See Devereux, *The Story of Wake Island,* for the information about Sergeants Wright and Godwin (p. 125), Corporal Miller (p. 144), Gunner McKinstry and Captain Platt (p. 188), Lieutenant McAlister (p. 190), Lieutenant Poindexter (p. 167), Corporal Brown (p. 162), Corporal McAnally (p. 160), Lieutenant Kliewer (p. 168), and Private First Class Breckenridge (p. 170); also for Devereux's remarks on morale (p. 143), the end of the air battle for Wake (p. 146), the mysterious light flashes (p. 147), the use of flamethrowers (p. 169), his description of the Japanese invasion (pp. 149-153, 161), and his discussion with Commander Cunningham of the possibility of surrender (pp. 174-175). The Japanese account of the landing is found in Devereux, p. 154. See Cunningham, *Wake Island Command*, for his report on the civilians who assisted in the defense of Wake (pp. 285-286), and his message to Admiral Pye that "the issue was in doubt" (p. 134). Morison, *The Rising Sun in the Pacific*, discusses the light flashes (p. 247), and the *Neches* (p. 243), and offers an excellent account of the indecision in Washington and at Pearl Harbor about the relief force (pp. 235-244, 249-254). Colonel Pfeiffer's account of the meeting with Admiral Pye about allowing the task force to proceed to Wake is from his interview with the USMC Oral History Program, pp. 178-179. The story about Major Putnam and the civilian construction workers is from Toland, *But Not in Shame*, p. 99. See Toland, *The Rising Sun*, for the attacks by Poindexter's and Putnam's forces, and for Devereux's message to Pearl about the enemy landing (pp. 101-104). In *The Defense of Wake*, Heinl discusses the light flashes (p. 40), the fighting at Lieutenant Hanna's position (p. 47), and the use of flamethrowers (p. 50). See Hough et al., *Pearl Harbor to Guadalcanal*, for information about ordering the submarines away from Wake (p. 131).

CHAPTER 8 *"The Death of Pride"*

See Devereux, *The Story of Wake Island*, for his account of Lieutenant McAlister's and Gunner McKinstry's attack (p. 192), and his conversation with Gunner Hamas and other reactions to the surrender (pp. 175-194); also his USMC Oral History Program interview, p. 124. See Toland, *The Rising Sun*, for anecdotes about Gunner McKinstry (p. 105), Lieutenant Poindexter (pp. 106, 108,

109), and Captain Platt (p. 109). Hough et al., *Pearl Harbor to Guadalcanal,* discusses Japanese losses in trying to take Major Putnam's position (p. 141).

CHAPTER 9 *"The Unknown Lay Ahead"*

See Devereux, *The Story of Wake Island,* for Gunner Hamas's account of imprisonment (p. 204), for the Japanese proclamation (p. 202), and for Devereux's interrogation by the Japanese (p. 207). See Cunningham, *Wake Island Command,* for his account of the early days of captivity (p. 146), and for his interrogation (pp. 144-146). See Toland, *The Rising Sun,* for information on the recall of the task force and the quotation from Tokyo Rose (p. 103). See Morison, *The Rising Sun in the Pacific,* for the dispatch from Admiral Pye (p. 253), the quotation from Admiral Reeves (p. 254), and the renaming of Wake Island by the Japanese (p. 254).

CHAPTER 10 *"Not Just Any Island"*

See Devereux, *The Story of Wake Island,* for his account of life in the POW camps and after the Japanese surrender (pp. 215-238). In *Wake Island Command,* Cunningham describes the brutality of Saito (p. 159). Enemy casualties are discussed in Heinl, *The Defense of Wake,* p. 67, and in Frank and Shaw, *Victory and Occupation,* p. 459. The surrender of Admiral Sakaibara to General Sanderson is described by Ernie Harwell in "The Wake story," *Leatherneck,* November 1945, pp. 22-26, and in "Wake revisited," in *The United States Marine Corps in World War II,* pp. 923-929.

EPILOGUE

The quotation is from Heinl, *The Defense of Wake,* p. 62.

APPENDIX II *The Cunningham Controversy*

The quotation from Hanson Baldwin is in his *The Crucial Years*, p. 382. The quotations from General Devereux are from his USMC Oral History Program interview, pp. 102, 113. All other quotations are from Cunningham, *Wake Island Command*, pp. 245, 253, 254, 259, 269, 271-273, 275, 277, 281, 287, 296-297, 299.

Sources

In addition to the books and articles listed below, a number of newspapers and popular magazines were consulted for the flavor of the times and the impact of the Wake Island story on the American people. These include the *New York Times, Washington Post, Time, Newsweek, Life,* and *Saturday Evening Post.*

In the military archives of the various services, materials examined included unit war diaries, action reports, casualty lists, personal narratives, fleet command summaries, dispatches, ship war diaries, and CincPac files. A valuable source of eyewitness impressions and observations is the Oral History Program of the Marine Corps' Historical Center.

BALDWIN, HANSON W. "The saga of Wake." *Virginia Quarterly Review* 18 (1942): 32.

————. *The Crucial Years: 1939-1941.* New York: Harper and Row, 1976.

BAYLER, WALTER L. J. *Last Man Off Wake Island.* Indianapolis: Bobbs-Merrill, 1943.

BURROUGHS, J. R. "The Siege of Wake Island," *American Heritage,* June 1959, pp. 65-76.

CUNNINGHAM, WINFIELD SCOTT. "The truth behind the Wake Island Marine hero hoax." *Cavalier,* May 1961, p. 10.

————. *Wake Island Command.* Boston: Little, Brown and Co., 1961.

DEVEREUX, JAMES P. S. *The Story of Wake Island.* Philadelphia: Lippincott, 1947.

DIERDORFF, ROSS. "Pioneer party—Wake Island." *United States Naval Institute Proceedings,* April 1943, pp. 499-508.

"Flame of glory: Wake's hopeless, gallant fight." *Time,* January 19, 1942, p. 20.

FRANK, BENIS M., and SHAW, HENRY I., JR., USMC Historical Section. *Victory and Occupation.* History of U.S. Marine Corps Operations in World War II, vol. 5. Washington, D.C.: Government Printing Office, 1968.

GREENE, FRANK L. *The Grumman F4F-3 Wildcat.* Profile 53. Windsor, England: Profile Publications Ltd., 1972.

HALSEY, W. F., and BRYAN, J. *Admiral Halsey's Story.* New York: McGraw-Hill, 1947.

HART, SCOTT. *Washington at War: 1941-1945.* Englewood Cliffs, New Jersey: Prentice-Hall, 1970.

HARWELL, ERNIE. "The Wake story." *Leatherneck,* November 1945, pp. 22-26.

———. "Wake revisited." In *The United States Marine Corps in World War II,* edited by S. Smith, pp. 923-29. New York: Random House, 1969.

HEINL, R. D., JR. "We're headed for Wake." *Marine Corps Gazette,* June 1946, pp. 35-38.

———. *The Defense of Wake.* Washington, D.C.: Historical Section, United States Marine Corps, 1947.

HOEHLING, A. A. *The Week Before Pearl Harbor.* New York: Norton, 1963.

HOUGH, FRANK O.; LUDWIG, VERLE E.; and SHAW, HENRY I., JR., USMC Historical Section. *Pearl Harbor to Guadalcanal.* History of U.S. Marine Corps Operations in World War II, vol. 1. Washington, D.C.: Government Printing Office, 1958.

"Isles of valor." *Newsweek,* January 5, 1942, p. 14.

LINGEMAN, RICHARD R. *Don't You Know There's a War On? The American Home Front, 1941-1945.* New York: Putnam, 1970.

MILLER, W. B. "Flying the Pacific." *National Geographic Magazine,* December 1936, pp. 665-707.

MONTROSS, LYNN. *The United States Marines.* New York: Bramhall House, 1959.

MORISON, SAMUEL ELIOT. *The Rising Sun in the Pacific, 1931-April 1942.* History of United States Naval Operations in World War II, vol. 3. Boston: Little, Brown and Co., 1963.

PERRETT, GEOFFREY. *Days of Sadness, Years of Triumph: The American People 1939-1945.* New York: Coward, McCann, 1973.

SHERROD, ROBERT. *History of Marine Corps Aviation in World War II.* Washington, D.C.: Combat Forces Press, 1952.

SMITH, S., ed. *The United States Marine Corps in World War II.* New York: Random House, 1969.

"Stand at Wake." *Time,* December 22, 1941, p. 19.

TOLAND, JOHN. *But Not in Shame: The Six Months After Pearl Harbor.* New York: Random House, 1961.

―――. *The Rising Sun: The Decline and Fall of the Japanese Empire 1936-1945.* New York: Random House, 1970.

UPDEGRAPH, CHARLES L., JR. *U.S. Marine Corps Special Units of World War II.* Marine Corps Historical Reference Pamphlet. Washington, D.C.: Historical Section, United States Marine Corps, 1972.

URWIN, GREGORY J. W. "The Wildcats of Wake Island." *Air Classics,* September 1977, pp. 76-82, 94-95.

"Wake's 378." *Time,* January 5, 1942, p. 20.

Index